Advertising Myths

The strange half-lives of images and commodities

Anne M. Cronin

 Routledge
Taylor & Francis Group

LONDON AND NEW YORK

First published 2004
by Routledge
11 New Fetter Lane, London EC4P 4EE

Simultaneously published in the USA and Canada
by Routledge
29 West 35th Street, New York, NY 10001

Routledge is an imprint of the Taylor & Francis Group

© 2004 Anne M. Cronin

Typeset in Times by Keystroke, Jacaranda Lodge, Wolverhampton
Printed and bound in Great Britain by The Cromwell Press, Trowbridge,
Wiltshire

British Library Cataloguing in Publication Data
A catalogue record for this book is available from the British Library

Library of Congress Cataloging in Publication Data
Cronin, Anne M., 1967–
     Advertising myths: the strange half-lives of images and commodities/
     Anne M. Cronin.
          p. cm. — (International library of sociology)
     Includes bibliographical references and index.
     1. Advertising—Social aspects. 2. Consumer behaviour.
     3. Consumption (Economics)—Social aspects. I. Title. II. Series.
     HF5821.C76 2004
     659.1′042—dc21   2003010028

ISBN 0–415–28173–3 (hbk)
ISBN 0–415–28174–1 (pbk)

Advertising Myths

Seer
adv
Cro
perf
clas
soci
betv
con
'cir
and
disti
alte
aca

Anr
Cul
Con

ςs,
Λ.
ιat
ιis
ιd
ns
ɔn
ɔy
ːrs
ɪg,
at
ιd

ʾor
ɪd

INTERNATIONAL LIBRARY OF SOCIOLOGY
Founded by Karl Mannheim

Editor: John Urry
Lancaster University

Contents

5 Advertising reconsidered   **113**

Figures

Acknowledgements

Many people have helped me in writing this book and I am very grateful for all their contributions. First and foremost, I would like to thank Claudia Casteñada and Imogen Tyler who offered support, intellectual commentary, and helped me see the wood for the trees in some of the trickier moments.

Many people at Lancaster University have contributed to the development of my ideas – and provided practical support in reading drafts and grant applications – but I would particularly like to thank Anne-Marie Fortier, Adrian Mackenzie, Jackie Stacey and John Urry. I have had many interesting discussions with Kevin Hetherington and Mimi Sheller about consumption and with Tim Hickman about the controveries over drugs and their consumption. Jane Kilby and Alan Warde read some wobbly drafts for me and provided invaluable comments. My thanks to all these.

Thanks also to Janine Grenfell and Beryl Vernon who supplied a lot of laughs as well as practical support, and to Damien Cashman for helping me with some technological queries. Thanks to all the advertising practitioners who agreed to be interviewed, and also to Geoff Russell of the Institute for Practitioners in Advertising, Claire Forbes of the Advertising Standards Authority and Tim Ambler of the London Business School.

I would also like to thank all the companies who kindly granted me permission to reproduce their images: Adbusters (http://adbusters.org), Gallaher Limited, the *Guardian*, Gucci, Imperial Tobacco Limited, Nike, V&S Vin & Sprit AB. I am also grateful to the World Health Organization and the artists Wim Delvoye, Komar and Melamid, and Lisa Milroy who allowed me to reproduce their work.

Thanks to people at Taylor and Francis, particularly Gerhard Boomgaarden, and also James McNally who untiringly answered a barrage of email queries from me.

I would also like to acknowledge the Arts and Humanties Research Board which provided me with a grant to complete this book (grant no. AN8471/APN13101).

Abbreviations

AA   Advertising Association [UK]
ASA   Advertising Standards Authority [UK]
ASH   Action on Smoking and Health [UK]
BACC   Broadcast Advertising Clearance Centre [UK]
BAT   British American Tobacco
CAP   Committee of Advertising Practice [UK]
EAAA   European Association of Advertising Agencies
EASA   European Advertising Standards Alliance
EAT   European Advertising Tripartite
FTC   Federal Trade Commission [USA]
IPA   Institute of Practitioners in Advertising [UK]
IAS   Institute of Alcohol Studies [UK]
ISBA   Incorporated Society of British Advertisers [UK]
ITC   Independent Television Commission [UK]
NAD   National Advertising Division [USA]
NARB   National Advertising Review Board [USA]
TMA   Tobacco Manufacturers' Association
WHO   World Health Organization

Introduction

For many years, advertising has excited the critical faculties of scholars as much as it has focused popular fascination and social censure. Classically, advertising has been seen as the primary social and commercial mediator between commodities and the consumer, products and society. For instance, Jhally (1987: 142) argues that, 'through advertising, goods are knitted into the fabric of social life and cultural significance'. In this understanding, advertising operates as a form of intermediary that translates material products into symbolic social entities and facilitates their integration into social networks of people, ideas, practices and institutions. Thus, predicated on its assumed powers to channel consumption practices, advertising has been considered a primary force that mediates social distinctions such as class, subculture, gender, nationality or age. Just as consumption acts are thought to reproduce social classifications and their complex inflection of power relations, advertising has been framed as the means of translating those capitalist ideals of incessant acquisition into individual consuming practices that conform to those social stratifications. *Advertising Myths* expands these understandings to consider the ways in which advertising operates to institute other forms of distinction such as those between the conceptual categories of 'person' and 'thing', consumer and commodity, and normal and 'dangerous' consumption.

In order to explore the contours of this formation, the book analyses the practices of the advertising industry, the textual artefacts or products of that industry, social responses to the dissemination of those products, and the controversies surrounding advertising as institution and as trope for contemporary society. In the long-running debates over these issues, advertising has frequently been framed as a manipulative force that fabricates or subverts the needs and desires of the individual. It was Galbraith who set the tone for many subsequent critiques of this type arguing that, 'many of the desires of the individual are no longer even evident to him. They have become so only as they are synthesized, elaborated, and nurtured by advertising and salesmanship, and these, in turn, have become among our most important and talented professions' (1958: 2). Beyond emphasising the fabrication of the consumer's repertoire of desires, this account also stresses the power of advertising as an institution and its practitioners' key role as cultural intermediaries. But very few subsequent studies have taken up this issue and engaged in a detailed analysis of the industry and advertising practitioners.[1] More commonly within academic analyses, an abstracted category of 'advertising' is put to work as a galvanizing trope that engenders generalized social and cultural criticism. Thus, advertising is used to illustrate a wide range of phenomena or is discursively employed as *evidence* of social change in debates such as those over the increasing significance of visual culture, the commodification of the social, the manipulative influence of television or the erosion of traditional social bonds. Advertising's ascribed function as index of the social derives from its purportedly isomorphic relationship to capitalism: advertising is imagined to reflect and disseminate the ideals of capitalism, whilst simultaneously *embodying* and performing the pernicious power of capitalist ideologies. Following this logic, Goldman (1992: 2) argues that the textual analysis of advertisements can 'map the cultural reproduction of commodity hegemony' and offer a precise cartographic transcription of capitalist society.

Part of the appeal of using advertising as a litmus test or index of society centres on the ubiquity of its texts. As Williamson (2000: 11) notes, 'even if you do not read a newspaper or watch television, the images posted over our urban surroundings are inescapable'. Whilst the pervasive quality of contemporary advertising has been the focus of much comment, I am particularly interested in the ubiquity of commentary upon, and critiques of, advertising. This constant rehearsal of ideas about advertising, and criticisms of its perceived effects, operate in multiple registers including that of popular enjoyment and critique, academic analysis, advertising agencies' own rhetoric about advertising, and regulatory and self-regulatory bodies. *Advertising Myths* focuses on the circulation of beliefs and understandings of advertising and asks how we license ourselves to make such claims about and through advertising. In this sense, I am taking an oblique stance in relation to the central debates around advertising, thus producing an ex-centric analysis. My account, therefore, does not rest on the thorny question of, 'does advertising work?'. This is generally framed in terms of an increase in product sales but, as I go on to argue, the question itself circulates within and beyond the industry as a constitutive 'myth'. My question is therefore formulated as, 'what is the work of advertising?' What is the nature of our investments in advertising and in analysing advertising? How does advertising operate as a taxonomy of the social? How does the circulation of understandings of advertising constitute that very 'persuasion industry'?

The title, *Advertising Myths*, refers to Roland Barthes' (1974) notion of myth elaborated in his classic study of advertisements and later taken up in other analyses such as that of Judith Williamson (2000 [1978]). For Barthes (1974: 129), 'myth is neither a lie nor a confession: it is an inflection'. Myth is not a concept, idea or object, and it does not operate through simple negation or deception – instead, 'myth is a system of communication' (Barthes 1974: 109). In his analysis of texts in general, and advertisements in particular, Barthes aims to show how myth purifies and naturalizes social phenomena, giving them an eternal and unquestionable justification. In this sense, myth does not operate through the denial of a social phenomenon, but rather through a continual elaboration and dissemination of understandings of that phenomenon. Through this mythologizing process, new articulations of social meanings are forged and naturalized whilst the very system of signification by which they were engendered is obscured and thus, 'things appear to mean something by themselves' (1974: 143). Barthes and later commentators use myth to analyse advertisements (textual artefacts) that are generally understood as the end-products of a long and often unstable process of the circulation of finance, regulatory strictures, beliefs about advertising, and their materialization in textual form. In my analysis, I am using myth to reference advertising as an entire institution not merely the textual end-products of its processes, and I am also departing from the classic sense that myth functions through naturalization. Instead, I argue that the complex circulation of beliefs and commercial imperatives acts to *constitute* the institution that is advertising. In parallel, I argue that advertising is used as a trope (by academics, by regulators, by advertising practitioners) for rehearsing understandings of the social and social relations. In this sense, advertising *itself* functions as a myth that circulates through multiple sites and articulates diverse commercial and political interests. It operates as a form of currency that constitutes the social order in discursive, material and economic ways but, in parallel, is also deployed as a trope or exemplar for analysing the social.

The book explores these flows of beliefs and interests by focusing on controversy about, and regulation of, advertising and takes as a specific case study the advertising of the 'dangerous commodities' of tobacco and alcohol. Using case studies of advertising, rather than presenting a broad account, offers a nuanced analysis of advertising processes and outcomes and avoids the tendency towards generalized claims about advertising's social and commercial impact. At the same time, the focus on issues of controversy distils more general perceptions about advertising, such as its manipulative powers and insidious reach, and thus presents a useful point of entry for the analysis of advertising in general. The sub-title of the book – *The strange half-lives of images and commodities* – resonates in (at least) three ways. First, the association of atomic half-life draws parallels with the way in which advertising is commonly imagined to erode the social, engendering a kind of radioactive decay as the traditional bonds of sociality are corrupted and increasingly replaced with a contaminated, commodified web of social relations. Goldman (1992: 8), for instance, argues that advertising has a 'dissolving influence on culture'. The case study of tobacco and alcohol advertising, with the associative ideas of risk, ill-health and addiction, further resonates with ideas of the erosion and contamination of both the individual subject and the social order. Furthermore, circulating understandings of 'dangerous consumption' extend beyond the central instances of addiction to substances such as alcohol and drugs and come to encompass other consuming practices such as shopping. In his classic account, Ewen (1988: 248) argues that contemporary capitalist societies are characterized by pathological consumption and 'the continuous cultivation of markets, obsessive/ compulsive shopping, and premeditated waste'. The 'half-life' of images is also intended to reference Appadurai's (1986) and Kopytoff's (1986) important analyses of commodities through the framework of 'the social life of things'. My approach to the circulation of beliefs about advertising resonates with their analysis of the biographies of commodities as they both flow between diverse sites and alter their symbolic status in the process: ads too have social lives. Advertisements' uncertain status as both material products and insubstantial, mobile signs casts their social lives as complex, protean and only half-appreciated. And lastly, the 'half-life' of images and commodities is intended to signal the way in which advertisements are commonly imagined to *animate* commodities, or at least the process by which commodities come into the lives of consumers. Advertising is thought to enliven the commodity, to spark an active relationship between consumer and commodity which reflects both on the agency and personhood of the subject and the ambiguous, animated, half-alive status of the commodity. This relationship is one of the central concerns of the book: I explore how myths of advertising constantly recount and rearticulate understandings of what it is to be a person by elaborating conceptual relationships to the categories of 'thing' and, more precisely, 'commodity'. The imagined animation of commodities by advertising troubles those distinctions between the categories of 'person' and 'thing' and becomes the site of controversy and regulation. Throughout the book, I examine how academic, popular and regulatory debates about the nature of advertising operate as circulating myths that constitute that taxonomic order and provide a lightning rod that channels a range of concerns about contemporary Euro-American societies.

In this analysis, I avoid making claims of grand epochal shifts in the realm of consumption and advertising. I am not suggesting that advertising today has reached its zenith of persuasive impact or social significance, nor that it embodies the very spirit of the moment. As Raymond Williams (1980) has noted, many historical periods have imagined themselves to be the age of advertising. Neither am I claiming that the controversies around advertising for 'dangerous' or addictive commodities such as tobacco and alcohol represent a new move to a 'culture of addiction': it is certainly not the case that the contemporary articulation of advertising and consumption represents a radical break with past formulations. Indeed, Foucault has argued that we must recognize that the time we live in is not '*the* unique or fundamental or irruptive point in history where everything is completed and begun again' (1990c: 36). Registering this caution, contemporary conceptualizations of advertising can nevertheless offer an important analytic site for tracking the development of particular modes of understanding the shifting classifications of 'person', 'commodity' and 'image'.

Chapter 1 situates these mutating categorizations within the context of nineteenth-century Euro-American societies. Whilst contemporary academic and popular accounts attribute considerable social power and commercial impact to advertising – thus framing it as key site of controversy – nineteenth-century perceptions held that advertising was significantly less influential. To examine this disjuncture, the chapter focuses on key consumption controversies of the period with a particular focus on the shifting classifications of kleptomania or oniomania (compulsive shopping). It analyses how the framing of such practices as deviant, and in some cases pathological, impacted upon the incipient norms of consumption in the new industrial societies. The unhealthy, pathological, or deviant bodies of kleptomaniacs and oniomaniacs became a source of fascination and contestation as well a site of social control – they became tropes for the elaboration of what it meant to be human in rapidly developing capitalist societies. As O'Connor argues,

The diseased body was symptomatic of the age: a focal point for both anxiety and exhilaration about the uncertain, shifting status of humanness in the age of capital, it imaged an emergent culture of surface, a world whose incipient modernity manifested itself not only in its penchant for making new identities, but also in its abiding fascination with watching itself make them.

(O'Connor 2000: 19)

Synchronous with this accent on the status of 'the person', these societies were fascinated by *things* in the form of collections, cluttered domestic interiors, museums, displays and exhibitions, and the new, mass-produced commodities (Briggs 1988; Olalquiaga 1999; Pearce 1992, 1995; Rabinbach 1992; Saisselin 1985; Seltzer 1992; Stewart 1993). The figures of the kleptomaniac and the onio-maniac embodied what were perceived as unhealthy or pathological relationships to commodities. These figures were strongly gendered and classed, representing the menacing erosion and reconstitution of gender and class boundaries and associated rights, and focused a range of anxieties about social change. By a process of contamination, the kleptomaniac and the oniomaniac were thought to constitute a danger to 'normal', respectable consumers by casting the new culture of com-modities in a dubious, threatening light. In this context, commodities came to be seen as 'strangely-animated objects' that acted independently of persons (Camhi 1993: 34).

Hence, the new framing of consuming practices through notions of addiction, compulsion and pathology became a key site through which the relations between the categories of 'thing' and 'person' were stated, rearticulated and policed. The causes of these consuming disorders were not attributed to advertisements but were distributed unevenly between the commodity or substance itself, the site or location (such as the department store), a weakness of individual will or moral debility, and biologically-inscribed tendencies. This causal emphasis stands in marked contrast to the way in which contemporary accounts stress advertising's central role in fostering unhealthy or negative relationships to commodities or consuming practices such as shopping. Despite these differences, important parallels exist between the functions of nineteenth-century and contemporary advertising and their respective definitions of deviant consumption. I argue that the 'pathological' consumption practices of the nineteenth century operated as classificatory devices or taxonomic tools, ordering the social and policing boundary infringements. This function is most evident in the distinctions instituted and reinforced between the conceptual categories of 'person' and 'thing', 'consumer' and 'commodity'. The developing commodity culture represented a challenge to those established taxonomies and channelled fears of a loss of humanity and human agency commensurate with the perceived growing power of the material world of things and commodities. Contemporary advertising, I suggest, operates in a manner parallel to those nineteenth-century conceptions in that it manages and rearticulates social clas-sifications. More broadly, it orders the conceptual distinctions between persons and things, generating a framework within which understandings of contemporary personhood are debated and institutionalized.

Chapter 2 focuses on contemporary UK regulation of advertising for 'dangerous commodities'. The processes by which the regulation was instituted in the UK in 2003, and the commercial responses it elicited, has gained a more pronounced significance in the context of the recent agreement of the global Framework Convention on Tobacco Control led by the World Health Organization.[2] Requiring a ban on tobacco advertising, this Convention recontextualizes to a global scale the issues, debates and controversies played out in the UK advertising (and tobacco) industry during the process of implementing regulation. Furthermore, exploring regulation offers a useful point of analytic access to the social and political concerns of any given period. In this chapter, I explore how these regulatory impulses and practices frame advertising as an animator of consumption processes, and how the institution of new regulations is motivated by an aim to redress the balance of power in the perceived dynamic tension between persons and things. To explore these issues, this chapter uses a case study of tobacco and alcohol advertising, but the scope of the analysis is not limited to advertising for 'dangerous commodities': a central element of my argument is that regulatory practices (and commercial practices aimed at deflecting regulation) dilate the definition of 'dangerous advertising' to the point that all advertising is perceived as (potentially) harmful or even socially pathogenic. The chapter tracks how regulatory institutions and practices form one element of the 'circuits of belief' in and about advertising and examines how each of the following frame understandings of advertising: regulatory bodies such as the Advertising Standards Authority and the Independent Television Commission; the advertising trade associations of the Institute for Practitioners in Advertising and the Advertising Association; non-governmental organizations such as the World Health Organization; UK legislative debates and bills, and European Union directives on advertising. The diverse understandings of the nature and function of advertising that circulate within and between these organizations figure advertising as textual artefact divorced from the complex flow of finance, practitioners' rhetoric, and commercial imperatives. I explore the consequences of such a focus on the apparent end-product of these processes and the unintended outcomes of the regulatory regimes. One of the ironies of the expansion of practices regulating advertising is the commensurate proliferation of alternative marketing practices designed to circumvent them. Arguably, these new marketing strategies, such as the 'brand experience' in sites such as airports, deploy novel and more finely-honed persuasion techniques that may have more of an impact upon consumers than the (now banned) conventional tobacco advertise-ments. In addition, by condensing concerns about advertising to the text of advertisements, regulatory moves paradoxically expand the scope of 'addictive' or dangerous consumption. Such drives do not merely repress or censor a social formation (in Foucault's terms, thus actively constituting them); they also function to disaggregate those dangerous practices and commodities and make them more fluidly mobile. By displacing the imagined site of pathology and addiction from the substance itself to its advertising – to the level of representation – the regulatory regimes ironically facilitate a wider circulation of those discourses and an associated proliferation of new hybrid forms of 'dangerous consumption'. Indeed, by accenting tobacco advertising's apparent disruption of type and classification (such as that of 'person' and 'commodity'), regulations amplify a sense that *all* advertising is dangerous and menaces the established ordering of the social.

Chapter 3 is based on interviews with advertising practitioners in London agencies. Slater (1989: 120) argues that advertising has most often been studied as a discreet set of texts or as a 'paradigm of communicative power' whilst less attention has been directed at the everyday processes and commercial interests of advertising agencies. This chapter addresses this omission by exploring the commercial imperatives of agencies and the personal investments of Creatives, Account Planners and Account Managers in the business of advertising. I argue that, contrary to the common perception of its commercial power, the advertising industry functions through a complex and provisional circulation of self-promotional rhetoric with short-term, ambiguous impact. Focusing on issues of controversial advertising and regulation, I explore the industry's practices and individual agencies' constant requirement to generate self-promotional rhetoric in a highly competitive field. I argue that the industry does not merely produce advertisements or 'commodity-signs'; agencies expend considerable effort and money in attempting to institute a system of commercial exchange based on their knowledge and skills. The circulation of these (self-) promotional accounts between agencies, their clients and regulators functions to *constitute* advertising as a social and economic form.

Chapter 4 examines advertising texts and compares them with health promotion campaigns and 'anti-advertisements' or 'subverts' produced by counter-cultural groups such as *Adbusters*. I explore how advertising is one part of a process of stabilization and destabilization of flows of beliefs, materialities and values into the commodity-form: advertising's textual form temporarily freezes a moment of those flows and makes certain values available for analysis. I examine how tobacco and alcohol advertising is imagined by critics and regulators to corrupt the correct or healthy flow of information between consumer and commodity. This is thought to produce maladies of textuality that must be addressed through an antidote of 'healthy' or corrective advertising in the form of anti-smoking/drinking campaigns. Expanding on these ideas, I explore how anti-smoking and drinking campaigns may function in ways contrary to those intended. Focusing on advertising's articulation of ownership and its conceptual rehearsal of the relationship between the categories of 'person' and 'thing', this chapter explores the paradoxes of contemporary advertising through a notion of a 'politics of synthetics'. Drawing on Marx's (1990) seminal accounts of the extraordinary amalgam of human labour-power and materiality that is the commodity, I argue that a 'politics of synthetics' represents the constitution or protean synthesis of the category of person in the play between notions of the animate and the inanimate form, the consumer and the commodity.

Chapter 5 draws together the arguments of the book and expands their scope by considering the contemporary proliferation of notions of consuming addictions or compulsions such as 'shopaholism'. I consider new ways of thinking about advertising, arguing that tracking the *circulation* of beliefs in and about advertising is key to fully apprehending it as a social and economic institution. Schudson (1993:

215) argues that advertising functions as a form of 'capitalist realism' that does not represent society *as it is*, but society *as it should be* according to capitalist ideals. Moving beyond Schudson's important account, I argue that advertising functions not only to present ideals of society but to construct new social taxonomies and new ways of instituting those classificatory regimes. Using Foucault's (1990a: 99) conceptualization of power–knowledge relations as 'matrices of transformations', I argue that advertising itself functions as a transformative matrix that re-orders social relations and contributes to the co-ordination of the relationship between the classifications of 'person' and 'thing'.

Throughout the writing of this book, I have been conscious of debates about the 'cultural turn' in academic analysis. For instance, Daniel Miller (2002) cautions that the current shift in the academic realm to analysing culture risks presupposing a commensurate shift in the world that academics are describing. In accenting the 'cultural' aspects of the industry – such as the circulation of beliefs and self-promotional rhetoric, and the work of advertising as classificatory matrix – I am aware of the danger of producing a self-fulfilling prophecy of culturalism. This I hope I have tempered with an attention to historical context and agencies' commercial imperatives. In a methodological vein, Lauren Berlant (2002) has commented that our questions at the start of a project are always bigger than our archive (or set of materials for analysis), and we therefore tend to reduce the scope of our questions to make them commensurate with that archive. To some extent, the questions directing my analysis have been gradually tailored throughout the writing process to correspond with the material available me. Highlighting these limitations, which I believe are inherent to most academic projects, works as a useful reminder of the necessarily restricted and partial account that any book can offer. *Advertising Myths* does not therefore claim to offer a definitive analysis of contemporary advertising but it does, I believe, offer insights into its complex commercial formations and its uneven, ambiguous impact upon the social. If advertising can be seen as a 'system of organized magic' (Williams 1980: 186), its alchemy may rest not in any manipulation of individuals' needs or desires, but rather in its status as a transformative matrix that orders the social by making and remaking distinctions between persons and our material world.

1 Images, commodities and compulsions

Consumption controversies of the nineteenth century

This chapter explores Euro-American nineteenth-century controversies centred on consumption, examines advertising's limited role in such controversies, and casts into relief contemporary concerns about consumption and advertising. By focusing on the discursive constitution of deviant or pathological forms of consumption such as kleptomania or oniomania (what we would now understand as compulsive shopping), I examine how new norms of consumption emerged in societies fascinated by *things*. This chapter does not represent a history of advertising or consumer culture; neither is it an aetiology of consumption understood as social pathogen – in some nineteenth-century accounts, consumption was certainly framed as pathological in its perceived threat to the social order and in its potential effects of social degeneration and moral decay. I am not aiming to reproduce those nineteenth-century understandings: this chapter does not suggest that consuming practices or advertisements engendered social decay or that the new culture of consumption should be understood as pathological. Rather, my aim is to produce a new synthesis of accounts of nineteenth-century consuming discourses that examines the apparently troubling and unstable relations between persons and commodities. The understanding that conceptual distinctions between persons and things are blurred has a long pedigree (see Kopytoff 1986), but it is in the nineteenth century that this porosity of boundaries comes to be seen as particularly problematic, taking its most potent form in controversies about commodities. Drawing on historians' accounts of such controversies, I offer a speculative account that explores the nineteenth century's rehearsal of the perceived relations between things, persons and images through emergent discourses of consuming compulsions. In this analytic synthesis, I displace nineteenth-century advertising from its conventionally-imagined status as key site of controversy and prime mediator of consumption acts by arguing that advertising was not at that time posited as a powerfully manipulative force. To explore the dynamics of those consuming controversies, I broaden my analysis to include an examination of the visual aspect and material form of the commodity. I conclude by arguing that whilst advertising and controversies about consumption were not held to have an intimate connection, they did share a common characteristic: both advertising and consuming controversies articulated nineteenth-century debates about type and classification, and focused powerful concerns about the erosion or displacement of established taxonomic hierarchies.

Walter Benjamin's (1973) characterization of the nineteenth-century *flâneur* condenses many of the themes that this chapter explores. For Benjamin, the figure of the *flâneur* encapsulated the shifting characteristics of urban life and the burgeoning of new sites of consumption; as he strolled through the crowded streets, the *flâneur* epitomized new sensory paradigms and etched out a new spatiality of the city.[1] In discussing Charles Baudelaire's poetry of nineteenth-century Parisian life, Benjamin wrote of the opiate-like effects of being part of a crowd – the experience of massed humanity numbed the pain and feelings of estrangement of those forced to live in the capital:

> The crowd is not only the newest asylum of outlaws; it is also the latest narcotic for those abandoned. The *flâneur* is someone abandoned in the crowd. In this he shares the situation of the commodity. He is not aware of this special situation, but this does not diminish its effects on him and it permeates him blissfully like a narcotic that can compensate him for many humiliations. The intoxication to which the *flâneur* surrenders is the intoxication of the commodity around which surges the stream of customers.
>
> (Benjamin 1973: 55)

The force of Benjamin's account does not simply derive from the joint role played by drugs and commodities in engendering Baudelaire's (1961) famous artificial paradises of intoxication and pleasure. Benjamin marshals the themes of the masses, intoxicating substances, the lure of the commodity and the ambiguous and disturbing relation between persons and things. These tropes were not merely coincident in the contemporary cultural landscape; they were cultural correlates that acquired a particular currency in late nineteenth-century Europe. Operating as social coefficients, they both drew together and amplified some of the major concerns of the period: the role intoxicating substances were thought to play in social degeneration; the effects of city life on the individual; the burgeoning culture of commodities; and massed groups of people which were increasingly framed as populations.

As Foucault (1990a: 139) has argued, this emphasis on the population was channelled through understandings of 'the species-body', that is, a new perception of the masses as a body of people. Such conceptual shifts facilitated a new form of social control or 'bio-politics of the population' which dealt with the 'propagation, births and mortality, the level of health, life expectancy and longevity, and with all the conditions that can cause these to vary' (ibid.). Through recasting the masses as a population, bodies and life itself became sites of social regulation in a new way. In effect, these new perceptual grids linked the body, consumption and population in explicit ways; they focused novel mandates for the control of individual consumption by drawing on new understandings of consumption's perceived significance at the level of the population, of the nation, of the species-body. But effecting social control through bio-politics was only part of late nineteenth-century regulatory concerns. In the previous quotation, Benjamin appears to suggest that the narcotic effect of the crowd is generated through the physical proximity and conceptual connection between people and substances, consumers and commodities. The individual caught up in the crowd both parallels the state of the commodity – thus creating a troubling consonance between person and thing – and is subject to the intoxicating lure of that commodity. This is indissociably a concern with the embodied experience of being part of an urban crowd – part of a mass focused around new sites of consumption – and the new modes of connection or forms of relationship with the commodity. Seen in this way, it is possible to suggest a nuanced version of Foucault's bio-politics that includes a politics of things or, more precisely, a politically charged concern with the forms of relationality between persons and things. This nineteenth-century politics of the non-biological, the inanimate, the 'not-living', draws its discursive force from the anxieties and fascination about the *relation* between persons and things; it is a relation which was articulated most forcefully and had most economic and social resonance through commodities and consumption.

Commodities, consuming pathologies and the useless object

Things, and particularly their consumption and display, were central to nineteenth-century culture (Briggs 1988). Museums ordered and displayed objects from around the world, hierarchizing and materializing European nations and their relation to 'uncivilized' cultures (Gosden and Knowles 2001; Pearce 1992, 1994, 1995). The medium of exhibition and spectacle grew in significance as a mode of relating to the material world and as a way of organizing the conceptual world (see Richards 1990). Commodities embodied imperial values and served as a currency for disseminating those values and expanding capitalism's material and ideological grasp (see McClintock 1995). Relationships to things took on intensified forms; the hobby of collecting, for instance, became a nineteenth-century passion and served as a means of ordering and controlling the natural and the social world (see Saisselin 1985; Stewart 1993). Taxidermy gained considerable cultural prominence as stuffed animals became popular commodities and the subject of collections. Elephants' feet were transformed into furniture, tiger jaws formed frames for clocks, hat stands were made from antlers, tiger and bear claws were fashioned into jewellery (Olalquiaga 1999). This was a fascination with things and, in the instance of animal-commodities, represented a fascination with the once-animate – the now-dead – available to be bought, collected and displayed. In this chapter, I am not attempting to review the considerable literature that explores the material culture of nineteenth-century Euro-America. Instead, I take as my focus nineteenth-century concerns about the relation between persons and things, and more precisely, the articulation of these anxieties in debates about, and regulation of, consuming practices. In parallel, I explore the process by which certain commodities and consuming practices came to be distanced from, and functioned as a contrasting definition for, 'normal consumption'. In the nineteenth century – the era which witnessed the mass production of commodities and a proliferation of technological inventions – novel goods and technologies were not uniformly greeted with consumers' delight. For some, 'the invasion of new things carried with it an element of threat' (Briggs 1988: 372). This apprehension, I will argue, derives not only from the threat of change or the disruptive influence of innovation, but also from the introduction of troubling alterations in the conceptual relationships between things and persons that these new objects engendered. Mechanical innovations distilled many of these anxieties: the perceived distinctions between the human and non-human were challenged or subjected to a process of erosion as the relays between persons and machines came to be conceived as more insistent – more as a relationship of kin than one of inventor or operator to inorganic mechanism (see O'Connor 2000; Rabinbach 1992; Seltzer 1992). But the issues of consumption and the contested nature of the commodity provided another key nexus of concern about this politically freighted relationship. Individual consumption and its supposed effects on the body was subjected to a bio-politics of control. In parallel, attempts to exert control over the perceived conceptual proximity of the category 'thing' to the category 'person' were instigated through the generation of taxonomic structures and collections. Nineteenth-century bourgeois culture had a fascination with objects which tended to manifest itself through 'bric-a-brac, clutter, accu-mulation' (Saisselin 1985: 65). Amidst this proliferation of objects, the production of a collection functioned to generate conceptual grids of seriality and classification, the appeal of which resided partly in their promise of affording some control over things (see Stewart 1993). Indeed, collecting was seen by some in the nineteenth century as a pathological form of consumption, symptomatic of modern malaises; in particular, collecting was cast as evidence of the unsettling power of objects over persons. In some accounts, however, collecting was seen less as evidence of objects' power over the consumer, or their desire to impose order on the masses of things, than as a sign of internal disorders of the individual. Here, Saisselin cites Paul Bourget's psychological essays of 1888 which defined collecting as,

> the refined mania of an unquiet period in which the fatigues of boredom and the diseases of the nervous sensibility led man to invent the factitious passion for collecting because his interior complexities made him incapable of appreciating the grand and simple sanity of things in the world around him.
>
> (cited in Saisselin 1985: 69)

In this account, the simple sanity of the natural order of things is disrupted by manias of taxonomy and the possession of objects. The interiority of the self is conceived in contradistinction to an exterior order of things: nervous disorders of the self exert their unruly influence and produce impulses to compromise the natural ordering of things in making a collection, that is, in producing new specifications of type and genre. Such anxieties about interior states were commonly expressed in the nineteenth century alongside 'a widespread fear that the energy of the mind and body was dissipating under the strain of modernity; that the will, the imagination, and especially the health of the nation was being squandered in wanton disregard of the body's physiological laws' (Rabinbach 1992: 6). Thus in nineteenth-century accounts, the imagined causes or locations of malady or social degeneration were multiple and often shifted uneasily within any one account. The causative emphasis was unevenly distributed between the social environment – such as crowded city life or the material effects of commodities – and the disturbed interior states or nervous disorders of the individual. In the following section, I explore in more depth one element of this nineteenth-century concern by focusing on the framing and acting out of the relations between persons and commodities in sites such as department stores, and in practices such as shopping, its illegal counterpart of shoplifting, and its pathologized form, kleptomania.

Nineteenth-century debates about commodities and consumption often took as their focus the department store. This is not to say that department stores dominated the retail environment: there were increasing numbers of 'multiples', analogous to contemporary chain stores, such as the London and Newcastle Tea Company which had between ten and twenty branches (Fraser 1981). These were stores of the mass market which stocked relatively cheap ranges of imported goods geared towards mass sale. In addition, co-operative societies played a significant role selling food and provisions in their stores (ibid.). But it was the department store that dominated the nineteenth-century imagination, inspiring writers such as Dreiser and Zola who located dramas of modernity, desire and pleasure in their extravagant interiors (Bowlby 1985). In practical terms, the department stores introduced new modes of retail, producing cheap versions of goods for the masses (Saisselin 1985). Goods were marked with a fixed price and customers were encouraged to browse through the stores and enjoy the carefully managed spectacle (Williams 1982). Indeed, historians suggest that what distinguished department stores from shops was primarily their 'invitation to desire' (Saisselin 1985: 33). The stores were designed to entertain and to encourage browsing and indeed came to be seen as almost magical spaces of the imagination 'where selling is mingled with amusement, where arousal of free-floating desire is as important as immediate purchase of particular items' (Williams 1982: 67).

Whilst department stores combined selling with entertainment in a novel, potent form, they also offered a new site in which different social groups could interact; the stores afforded a quasi-respectable public space in which women and men, as well as different social classes, could mingle. This cultural shift elicited a range of criticisms from nineteenth-century commentators who articulated concerns about threats to class and gender boundaries (Tiersten 2001). This new social space was a worrisome development for some, representing an erosion of the social order, potentially endangering the morals of ladies, and creating the possibility of shifts in class position. For example, the shopgirl in the department store represented 'the hope of social mobility for the daughters of the lower middle classes on the one hand, and the moral depravity of these frenetic and seductive workplaces for reformers on the other' (Crossick and Jaumain 1999: 31). For ladies, the possibilities of shopping in these new urban spaces offered the erotic frisson of newly authorized public encounters with men as well as the intensified pleasures of luxury and possession (Tiersten 1999). One threat of consumer culture was thus the way in which it appeared to offer women forms of independence that undermined their traditional roles within the family (Tiersten 2001). However, the developing consumer culture of the nineteenth century and the advent of the department store in

Euro-American societies did not represent entirely new connections between women, shopping and ideas of luxurious consumption. These links can be traced back at least to the early eighteenth century when women were seen as the driving forces in the demand for luxury and expense and were censured for indulging in impulsive spending (Crossick and Jaumain 1999). But the department store of the nineteenth century provided a new context for these associations, creating a densely charged environment of commodified display that engendered 'popular and accessible models of sexual identity and conduct [and] reformulated and gave specific meanings . . . to definitions of manhood and womanhood, and to models of heterosocial and heterosexual interaction' (Reekie 1993: xix).

The development of the department store channelled a range of criticisms that were paralleled in concerns about new pathologies associated with the use of certain substances. Running alongside more established conceptual paradigms such as diseases of the will or nerve-power, the new concept of addiction was beginning to frame certain understandings of the consumption of alcohol and drugs such as morphine (see Valverde 1998). In parallel, the opulence and sensuousness of the displays in department stores was thought to overwhelm weak-willed persons (Miller 1981). In 1904, Theodore Dreiser wrote of New York's store windows: 'what a stinging, quivering zest they display . . . stirring up in onlookers the desire to secure but a minor part of what they see, the taste of a vibrating presence, and the picture that it makes' (cited in Leach 1989: 99). Indeed, the stores used display to create 'a visual vocabulary of desire' (Leach 1989: 103), and it was women and the lower orders who were thought to be particularly susceptible to their allure (Miller 1981). Writing in 1882, one critic described the department store as a mass of 'intoxicating displays, the shimmer of fabrics, dazzling mirages, irresistible seductions . . . which bedazzle women' (cited in Tiersten 1999: 122). This heady mixture led the department store to be seen as 'a crucible of new urban pathologies' focusing a range of social concerns (Tiersten 1999: 120). In this new context, women who purchased goods and, as we shall see, women who stole merchandise, were responding to 'the calculated arousal of desire in an environment dedicated to sensory stimulation and unfettered abundance' (Abelson 1989: 11). The new culture of consuming – epitomized by the department store and the consumption of alcohol and drugs – was thought to introduce retrograde social shifts and precipitate the degeneration of self and social structure. Both articulated anxieties about the disintegration of class structure and blurring of gender roles. For instance, the regulation of substances was a consequence 'not of their pharmacology, but of their association with social groups that were perceived as potentially dangerous' (Kohn 1992: 2). In nineteenth-century Britain, conceptions of particular substances were closely tied to the perceived status and social role of women, the working classes, and to issues of race and empire. Hence, driven by the ideal of mental hygiene, public health measures focused on the problematic use of alcohol, an issue which was also discussed in synonymous terms with concerns about racial dilution and pathology and national decline (McDonald 1994). In these debates about the effects of alcohol, 'women became the focal point for many of the proposed measures to counteract the increasing "degeneracy of the race"' (Thom 1994: 34–5).

In this way, classifications of race, gender, class and nationality functioned as primary points of articulation for nineteenth-century perceptions of 'dangerous consumption'. In effect, the more that the working classes, black people, Catholics and Irish immigrants were perceived to be heavy drinkers, the more drinking was perceived to be a problem (McDonald 1994). In this controversy, compromised will or nerve-power, or unbalanced ratios of will to desire, were considered to contribute to problematic consumption of substances (Valverde 1998). This is was what Valverde (1998: 67) calls 'the social stratification of the free will', that is, a classifying structure which posits women and lower class groups as inherently lacking will. In this context, it is clear that the laws and regulations governing 'dangerous substances' were primarily concerned with governing the realm of freedom (ibid.). These forms of social control, I suggest, do not concern themselves solely with the ingestion of dangerous substances and the morally and socially atrophying effects thought to result from this; they also attempted to govern the more general realm of consumption, delimiting it as an important nexus of individual action, social stratification and cultural taxonomy.

I am not suggesting that we should collapse nineteenth-century concerns with commodities and shopping with concerns about alcohol and drugs (see Cronin 2002a). Instead, I wish to explore how the contours of those discourses – the consumption of commodities and the ingestion drugs and alcohol – formed a consonance with one another, each drawing on the other's conceptual frameworks to cohere into powerful discursive forms that took a firm hold of the nineteenth-century imagination. In the regulatory project around drugs and alcohol, 'moral and political perceptions of danger allowed and encouraged the establishment of a pharmacology of harm' (McDonald 1994: 4). Nineteenth-century commentators deployed these tropes of intoxication and unhealthy connection to substances to describe the forms of sensory stimulation engendered by the department store and the lure of the commodity. One journalist of the time wrote that shoppers emerging from department stores appeared to 'wear a bizarre expression. Their pupils were extraordinarily dilated . . . and they have dark shadows beneath their eyes' (cited in Tiersten 1999: 121). The same journalist argued that 'bourgeois shoppers were subject to "new styles of neurosis"' (Tiersten 1999: 120–1). In effect, these new patterns of behaviour and new sensory paradigms were being pathologized in attempts to understand the appeal of this new form of consumer culture: 'the sheer excitement of shopping, it was claimed, became a drug to which once responsible bourgeois wives became addicted' (Crossick and Jaumain 1999: 31). Indeed, many contemporary academic accounts of the perceived compulsion of nineteenth-century consumer culture are written in today's vocabulary of addiction. For example, the consumer – typified by the middle class woman – came to be seen as a 'shopping addict and impulsive spendthrift' (Tiersten 1999: 122) and became 'addicted to cheapness' (Spiekermann 1999: 141). These tropes of addiction hold great resonance for contemporary Western subjects in the context of a proliferation of addiction-attribution – the concept of addiction is today used to frame a vast range of practices such as exercise or sex (see Sedgwick 1994). Yet the deployment of the concept of addiction to frame nineteenth-century understandings of consuming practices is rather anachronistic. Addiction as a concept was not firmly established in either medical or popular discourses of the time; it was only just developing at this period and overlapped with a range of other understandings of consumption pathologies as forms of mania, neurasthenia (a chronic form of mental fatigue) or particular forms of hysteria (Valverde 1998).

My interest lies in how discourses of consumption and those of compulsion and addiction co-mingled to produce a powerful conceptual field through which substances, commodities and practices came to be understood. These discourses coalesced in multiple forms, including those of oniomania (now cast as compulsive shopping) and kleptomania which drew on a sense of self with psychological depths: 'along with alcoholism, prostitution, and other forms of criminality, shopping infractions came to be perceived less as manifestations of flawed character than as symptoms of psychic debilitation, to be studied and managed by scientific experts' (Tiersten 2001: 46–7). In 1816, a Swiss doctor called André Matthey codified a mania for theft as 'klopémanie' and by the 1830s the usage of the term had become quite widespread (Pinch 1998: 124). Indeed, during the nineteenth century the concept of kleptomania became established across Europe and America partly as a way of legitimizing the new discipline of psychiatry which gained a high profile in providing expert testimony in law courts (O'Brien 1983). The conception of stealing as a form of madness had been circulating since at least the eighteenth century, but the nineteenth-century emergence of kleptomania signalled a new medicalization of shoplifting which articulated with perceptions of the developing consumer culture. The debate over the causes of kleptomania was fragmented and contradictory, but generally its causes were attributed both to the social environment – such as the site of the department store and the lure of the commodity – and to individual pathology which was often framed as a weakness of the will (Spiekermann 1999). On a social level, the department stores were considered dangerous places that were, in the words of a nineteenth-century critic, 'apéritifs of crime' that incited overwhelming desires for commodities which could ultimately be satisfied only by stealing (cited in O'Brien 1983: 73). On an individual level, the primary cause of kleptomania was considered to be a loss of reason as stealing what one did not need was thought to be irrational. As irrationality had long been associated with women (see Diprose 1994; Felski 1995; Pateman 1988), this connection was one which convincingly married the logics of irrationality, the lure of consumer culture and perceptions of women's physiology in the minds of contemporary writers and the new profession of psychiatry. Kleptomania came to be firmly linked to female physiology such that women were thought to be particularly susceptible during menstruation, pregnancy and menopause, all thought symptomatic of women's 'auto-toxic condition' (O'Brien 1983: 68). In effect, women were being poisoned or drugged by their own bodies: women were victims of their own pathology, a natural pathology of the female body. One nineteenth-century French doctor produced a study of such conditions:

> For Dr. Dubuisson, the pathological consumer was qualitatively different from a 'normal' one: the kleptomaniac, he wrote, was incited to action by an

irresistable drive or impulse absent in most women. From 120 cases of theft, he found nine garden-variety thieves and 111 'femmes coquettes', who suffered from the *monomanie de vol* [monomania of theft]. Among these, he diagnosed 33 cases of pure 'mental troubles', ranging from delirium to dull-wittedness, 26 cases of 'moral or physical exhaustion', including neurasthenia and other nervous disorders, and 52 'maladies of the nervous system', including hysteria, pregnancy, and menstruation. In 78 cases, he linked pathological behaviour directly to biological dysfunction.

(Tiersten 2001: 48–9)

Shopping and consuming pathologies came to be so closely associated with women that by the turn of the century in Germany, theft in department stores came to be seen as a 'special form of sex crime' (Spiekermann 1999: 149). This can be understood in multiple senses: as a new psychiatric definition of sexual pathology; as a focus on the perceived sexual allure of the department stores; and in the sense that women as a sex were thought to be the primary victims/criminals in this behaviour. Articulating with the perceived biological imperatives inherent in sexual difference, the social stratification of class was key in defining the pathology of kleptomania as distinct from shoplifting ('normal' or common stealing). The shock and moral outrage in discovering wealthy and middle-class women stealing from department stores was evident in nineteenth-century accounts. One such commentator wrote,

> It should appear to a stranger from another hemisphere a strange thing that we should boast of our Christian civilization, while we had such as spectacle as was seen even at a later time than this. – An elderly lady, of good station and fortune, might be seen on the treadwheel in Cold Bath Fields prison, in the jail-dress, and with her hair cut close – for the offense of shoplifting. It is difficult to write this fact; and it must be painful to read it; but the truths of the time must be told.

(cited in Pinch 1998: 125)

But middle- and upper-class women who were caught stealing from department stores were only rarely handed over to the police and were instead dealt with informally by store detectives (Spiekermann 1999). As it was considered morally unfeasible for middle- and upper-class women to be common thieves, the medicalized concept of kleptomania was used as explanation and justification for their behaviour (Abelson 1989). Indeed, kleptomania was frequently used as a defence during trials of middle-class women accused of shoplifting and almost always secured a lenient verdict (O'Brien 1983).

Thus nineteenth-century debates and controversies over shopping and stealing commodities articulated the parameters of acceptable or normal consumption alongside appropriate gender and class characteristics and boundaries. In particular, the idea of 'the useless object' distilled contemporary thinking about gender, commodities and the lure of possession. For instance, department stores were thought to foster 'an extravagant taste not only for clothes but also for "things one might do without"' (Saisselin 1985: 62). In parallel, the newly medicalized form of stealing relied on notions of utility and longing. Citing a French psychiatry manual of 1903, O'Brien argues that after 1880, 'kleptomania was recognised almost universally as a "morbid impulse to steal perfectly useless objects or those that could easily be paid for"' (1983: 67). Indeed, O'Brien suggests that the distinctive feature of the new consumer culture was less the purchase or use of goods than the *possession* of them. Central to this paradigm of consumerist possession was its partner in crime – kleptomania – which shared the same possessive urge whilst employing rather different methods of acquisition. Kleptomania was key in etching out understandings of the consumerist desire for possession, for 'if kleptomaniacs were stealing apparently useless goods, did that not also mean that many honest women were buying them?' (O'Brien 1983: 72). One nineteenth-century 'victim' of kleptomania described herself as gripped or possessed by the desire for goods in a frenzied state akin to drunkenness:

> I felt myself overcome little by little by a disorder that can only be compared to that of drunkenness, with the dizziness and *excitation* that are peculiar to it. I saw things as if through a cloud, everything stimulated my desire and assumed, for me, an extraordinary attraction. I felt myself swept along towards them and I grabbed hold of things without any outside and superior consideration intervening to hold me back. Moreover I took things at random, useless and worthless articles as well as useful and expensive articles. It was like a monomania of possession.
>
> (cited in Miller 1981: 202–3, emphasis in original)

Hillel Schwartz (1989: 416) suggests that the department stores played on this sensory arousal in that they 'operated on the contradictory axioms that no desire is unfulfillable and that no desire can be satisfied'. In this understanding, kleptomania was the unintended but unavoidable counterpart to the desire to buy which was cultivated at great expense by the stores. Writing of contemporary society, Haug (1986) suggests that shoplifting can be seen as an important index of the commodity's appeal because,

> the functional complex of commodity aesthetics is meant to trigger off the act of buying as forcefully as possible. Its functional ideal would be the compulsion to buy, but it is not capable of this directly . . . But if the 'desire to buy' could be induced directly, there would be no shoplifting problem. Commodity aesthetics fulfils its function only via needs, which it must channel towards a certain commodity, and whip up into a compulsive intensity. The success of commodity aesthetics is the specific need, which irresistibly demands the acquisition of the 'courted' commodity. The form of acquisition remains indeterminate. . . . Thus not only the sales figures but also the theft rates are seen as an achievement of commodity aesthetics.
>
> (Haug 1986: 39)

Haug proposes that capitalism succeeds in stimulating longing for all manner of 'useful' and 'useless' commodities but that these unleashed desires cannot always be directly channelled into the purchase of that commodity: those whetted appetites may also become misdirected and translated into practices of shoplifting. Hence, the power of commodity aesthetics may be gauged not only by the purchase of goods but also by the incidence of their theft. Whilst a rather schematic account – that problematically personifies and grants agency to 'commodity aesthetics' or capitalism – Haug's argument does point to a contemporary articulation of what many historical analyses outline: the new norms of nineteenth-century consuming were defined in articulation with the deviant forms of stealing, the pathologized form of kleptomania, and oniomania. Kleptomania and oniomania operated as measures of the new consuming society and women's place in it. The new spaces of consumption such as department stores with their characteristics of display, luxury and abundance were defined in opposition to an ethos of utility. Neither were the consumption patterns of purchase and theft that they elicited circumscribed by notions of need and use-value. The objects of the possessive desire of the kleptomaniac were primarily 'useless' or frivolous goods relating to feminine adornment; gloves, ribbons, stockings, lace, silk, combs. Camhi (1993: 33) argues that in focusing on these prostheses of classed, feminine identity, female klepto-maniacs can be understood to be acting out the conventional logics of women's social roles, now attached to commodity culture in a newly intensified way: 'like the hysteric, the department store kleptomaniac merely took a socially prescribed norm of feminine sexuality to its extreme (but nevertheless intrinsic) conclusion: the female consumer denuded of resistance, feminine sexuality entirely formed and possessed by the fetishized commodities sold to create it'. Of course, this account should not be taken as representative of nineteenth-century women's actual consumption patterns or sense of self. However, Camhi's analysis strikingly illus-trates how the nineteenth-century imagination emblematically employed the figure of woman in order to reflect on social change and commodity culture.

> As consumption migrated ever closer to the center of social identity, the kleptomaniac presented the spectacle of a thoroughly modern subject, without the slightest hint of a barrier intervening between herself and the marketplace of goods. The anxieties of an emerging culture of consumption invested her pathological image: the fear that strangely-animated objects directed the consumers' desires, and that consumption itself, last bastion of individual perogative in an increasingly-regulated industrial society, was entirely deter-mined by the marketplace of goods.
>
> (Camhi 1993: 34)

But can we say that consumption was seen as an established arena of individual prerogative in the nineteenth century? Was it perceived as a privileged zone of individual agency to be defended against the assault of industrial market society? As Camhi notes, the nineteenth-century culture of consumption was in an emergent, fledgling form. It was in a process of gradually weaving together its characteristics out of the many discourses of selfhood, hedonism, exchange and possession that were circulating at the period (see Campbell 1987). Camhi's account glosses over how the very notion of a culture of consumption emerged in fusion with eighteenth- and nineteenth-century debates on freedom, will and pleasure. It is, however, possible to say that the perception of consumption as a realm of freedom emerged in articulation with consuming deviances such as kleptomania, but one set of discourses did not precede or determine the other. Additionally, as I have noted above, the perceived causes of consuming compulsions were multiple and at times contradictory, thus defusing the potential of the kleptomaniac to unambiguously symbolize or channel nineteenth-century cultural fears: the sources of 'diseases of the will' (Valverde 1998) such as inebriety, kleptomania and compulsive shopping were highly debated and contested. Indeed, kleptomania was only one of many competing accounts of deviant behaviour such as partial insanity, moral insanity and monomania which circulated and bled into one another (Schwartz 1989). But central to my analysis is the way in which the attribution of cause shifted between the material properties of the substance or site itself (alcohol, opium, the commodity, the department store) and the nature of the self (lack of will, female biological propensity, overabundance of desire, moral debility). Thus, in addition to the suspect biology of female consumers, a range of other factors vied for causal status. The physical setting of the department store, for instance, was seen as a key motivating force for theft which was 'attributed to the new and dangerous availability of consumer goods in a deregulated and morally disintegrating modern world' (Felski 1995: 69). Paralleling concerns about drug and alcohol consumption, department stores were blamed for unsettling and blurring the boundaries between the deviant (which had increasingly come to be defined as the pathological) and the normal. The deviant working-class shoplifter, the middle-class kleptomaniac, and the respectable customer were shockingly united in their 'common capitulation to the lure of the commodity' (Felski 1995: 69). Thus, causes of shoplifting were seen by some medical commentators as 'the inevitable con-sequence of prolonged exposure to the department store' (Tiersten 2001: 49). The commodity itself was also subjected to criticism for exciting possessive passions through the appeal of its material form. For instance, the figure of the 'palpeuse', who was drawn to fondle the merchandise in department stores, became well known (Tiersten 1999: 123).

In all, there were multiple and competing nineteenth-century accounts of consuming practices which pinpointed causal influences in many different sites. To further complicate the picture, these conceptual frameworks were unevenly adopted. For instance, in line with incipient nineteenth-century discourses of drug and alcohol addiction, kleptomania was never a unified explanatory category or regulatory force. In many European countries, the concept of kleptomania had become rather out of fashion in medical discourse by the 1890s (Spiekermann 1999), although it retained its importance in popular and journalistic accounts. One parallel explanation argued that in stealing there was no independent pathological mania and that theft should be seen not as 'a compulsive act' but rather as a criminal act, 'committed in a state of impaired consciousness' (Spiekermann 1999: 145).

Thus, the shifting attribution of deviance or pathology between various sites, substances, and mental and biological states created a complex web of perceived causes that did not focus solely on the body. As Foucault has argued, the understanding of the body as origin or cause of disease or pathology is a relatively recent medical development:

> the space of *configuration* of the disease and the space of *localization* of the illness in the body have been superimposed, in medical experience, for only a relatively short period of time – the period that coincides with nineteenth century medicine and the privileges accorded to pathological anatomy.
>
> (Foucault 2000a: 3–4, emphasis in original)

As I have argued, the origins or causes of consuming compulsions were not only located within the space of the body; these attributed causes were multiple, unevenly applied, and vied with each other for prominence in nineteenth-century understandings.

Just as the norm of the consuming subject was in the process of being delineated, so also was the notion of the criminal subject and 'the dangerous individual'. Foucault (1990c: 132) identifies a key shift in nineteenth-century conceptions of criminality, insanity and the concept of 'the legally responsible agent'. Previously, emphasis was placed squarely on the crime itself, but during the nineteenth century attention also came to focus on a troubling element of the social body which was signalled by the crime – 'the dangerous individual' (ibid.). Foucault (1990c: 144) identifies the establishment of a technical knowledge-system which was capable of 'characterizing a criminal individual in himself and in a sense beneath his acts; a knowledge-system able to measure the index of danger present in an individual; a knowledge-system which might establish the protection necessary in the face of such a danger'. This social shift incorporated a sense of differentiation in which people were individuated in terms of their character and their acts. Simultaneously, the new form of control of 'the population' through bio-politics subjected such individuals to regulation and enforced regimes of treatment. In this context, conditions such as insanity or forms of mania came to be perceived as a danger to that individual but also (through understandings of heredity) represented a threat to society as a whole. This incipient conception of the self was characterized by psychological depths or a form of interiority that, in turn, had particular consequences for the framing of new consuming disorders such as kleptomania or compulsive purchasing: 'the more the act is, so to speak, gratuitous and undetermined, the more it will tend to be excused. A paradox, then: the legal freedom of a subject is proven by the fact that his act is seen as unnecessary' (Foucault 1990c: 140). Hence, the middle- or upper-class woman who stole from a department store could be defined as legally non-responsible because she could easily afford and hence did not *need* to steal the commodities in question – this framed her diagnosis as a kleptomaniac rather than a common shoplifter or thief. In contrast, this framework figured the working-class woman who stole as directed by principles of utility and circumstances of want. In effect, her economic status and thus her limited access to the market defined the terms of her legal responsibility and her (legal) mental state.

Foucault's highly influential analysis focuses on the new significance of the individuated subject and his/her perceived role in maintaining social cohesion or contributing to social degeneration. But Foucault (1990c) was careful not to frame his analysis in terms of a radical displacement of regulatory attention from the crime to the identity of the criminal: these concerns, he argued, ran in parallel and shared an equally weighted significance. Thus, in Foucault's own terms, nineteenth-century discourses were not uniquely centred on inventing the psychological depths of a subject or on creating taxonomies of social identity ('the criminal' or 'the homosexual', for example). Coexistent powerful discourses conceived subjects not as units of psychological interiority but as bodies of dumb mass (O'Connor 2000). Alternative nineteenth-century understandings conceived persons as embodied forms that transmitted 'organic memory' across generations through their very fleshy materiality rather than through consciousness or patterns of social identity (Otis 1994: 3). In the context of my own analysis of consumption, I would like to supplement the conceptual scope of the analysis outlined by Foucault. In accounts of nineteenth-century consumption disorders such as oniomania (shopping mania) or kleptomania, it is certainly possible to track how causes of deviance, mental or emotional disorder, and bodily pathology were unevenly and unsystematically attributed to the substance (drug or material form of the commodity), the site (the department store, for example), the biological imperatives of the body, or the individual will. As I have argued, there was no overarching perception of cause. I would also suggest that Foucault's account of bio-politics should be supplemented by a politics of things, or to be more accurate, a politics of the perceived relationality between persons and things, consumers and commodities. My synthesis of historical accounts indicates that nineteenth-century Euro-American cultures did not concern themselves solely with the bio-logics of population and control of life at the level of the species-being. Those societies also surveilled and regulated the logics of person–thing relations and, most especially, focused on the relations between persons and commodities in the burgeoning consumer capitalism. In Chapters 4 and 5, I call these forms of relationship a 'politics of synthetics' and expand upon how the classifications of 'the person', and particularly 'the consumer', are imagined and 'substantialized' through that relationship.

In contemporary western societies, it has become usual to conceive these relations in terms of capitalist mediation and it is, of course, advertising that is thought to function in the primary mediating role. Advertising is conventionally imagined to reach out to the potential consumer, make a connection, and thus stimulate desire for a commodity. This connective relation between commodities and persons is generally perceived today as manipulative or at least highly persuasive. As I argue in Chapter 2, advertising tends to be framed as an efficient commercial propaganda tool which serves capitalist interests by stimulating sales and producing a favourable consuming attitude amongst the population. In contrast, nineteenth-century advertising was not generally attributed these manipulative powers and the criticisms of advertising and the regulations put in place tended to reflect this. The following section explores nineteenth-century understandings of advertising and expands the scope of the analysis to consider 'the dialectical image'.

Advertising and the dialectical image

There is a wide-ranging literature which tracks the rise of advertising in Euro-American societies in the nineteenth and early twentieth centuries (e.g. Elliott 1962; Garvey 1996; Hower 1949; Laird 1998; Loeb 1994; Nevett 1982; Ohmann 1996; Pope 1983; Presbrey 1929; Richards 1990; Turner 1965). Such accounts emphasize the rapid increase in the volume of advertisements; for example, after 1848 new printing processes enabled the relatively cheap production of 10,000 billposter sheets an hour and by 1885, there were 522 billposter firms operating in 447 towns in Britain (Fraser 1981). Indeed, developments in mass printing technologies for newspapers and magazines afforded more sites for advertising and more opportunities to refine its forms and techniques (Garvey 1996). In parallel, advertising agencies grew in number, expanding their media space-selling remit to include research and creative input, and developed their expertise in new forms of promotion (Ohmann 1996; Pope 1983). The new, expanded role of agencies meant increased numbers of advertising practitioners, but as Lears (1983: 17) argues, they were a diverse group with a range of different beliefs and motivations: 'some were cynical manipulators; others were prophets of abundance deluded by their own ideologies; still others were uncertain seekers groping for secure identities in a rationalizing culture'. These accounts also emphasize an array of social effects: advertising played on its perceived transformative power (Loeb 1994; Richards 1990); it mediated fantasies of democracy (Loeb 1994); it fragmented the self, reducing it to a series of consumption acts (Richards 1990). Moreover, advertising presented a 'civilized morality' of self-control alongside its promotion of a fascination with the exotic and the primitive (Lears 1994: 144), and it functioned to 'mediate the Victorian poetics of racial hygiene and imperial progress' (McClintock 1995: 209).

My interest here does not lie in rehearsing these arguments, nor in attempting to remap advertising's history. Rather, I aim to explore how nineteenth-century views of advertising articulated some specific social concerns and ideals. As I outline more fully in Chapter 2, nineteenth-century attacks on advertising, or attempts to regulate advertising, tended not to attribute to advertising highly persuasive or manipulative powers. Rather, criticisms were channelled into perceptions of bill-posting as a polluter of public space which created aesthetically displeasing cityscapes and rural landscapes. Indeed, there were few supporters of street advertising with the notable exception of Oscar Wilde who defended billposters, 'as they bring colour into the drab monotony of the English streets (cited in Elliott 1962: 165). Other criticisms focused on patent medicine advertising which constituted 25 per cent of all advertisements by 1880 (Loeb 1994). One Harvard psychologist in 1894 complained that patent medicine advertisements were, 'the medical advertisement abomination' and argued that 'the authors of these advertisements should be treated as public enemies and have no mercy shown' (cited in

Laird 1998: 235). Attacks highlighted the dubious ingredients of patent medicines and their extravagent claims, drawing a great deal of critical attention to advertising in general: 'as the most visible and most objectionable single category of advertiser (since alcohol advertisements rarely reached into bourgeois homes), the patent medicine promoters drew negative attention to the entire practice of advertising, and the aspersions cast on them spread to the entire field' (Laird 1998: 236). Yet still these criticisms were not directed at a sense that advertising *manipulated* the consumer and this stands in marked contrast to contemporary views that often attribute enormous persuasive powers to advertising. For although nineteenth-century critics thought that patent medicine advertisements consisted of 'outrageous fictions', they considered that the chief problem lay not with advertising itself, but rather with the inherent weakness and gullibility of the masses (Richards 1990: 183). Even manufacturers were unconvinced about advertising's persuasive potential or commercial efficacy in promoting their products. In pre-1890 USA, advertising was not widely accepted as a necessary part of commercial endeavours (Hower 1949). Hower argues that this situation altered substantially between 1900 and 1910, citing one advertising practitioner in the trade paper *Printer's Ink* in 1910: 'twenty-five years ago it was hard to convince a man that advertising could be made to pay. Today the hardest thing we have to do, at times, is to make a prospective advertiser understand advertising limitations and successfully insist upon getting the matter right' (cited in Hower 1949: 229).

The precise periodization of this shift in the perception of advertising's commercial legitimacy can be debated, but it is certain that contemporary under-standings of the power of advertising to influence minds is radically different to most nineteenth-century understandings. Most significant for my analysis is the way in which advertising gradually came to be seen as a prime medium for negotiating the relations between persons and things, and thus for delimiting and characterizing the category 'person'. For instance, in his influential study of American advertising between 1880 and 1930, T.J. Jackson Lears (1983: 16) argues that advertising – and particularly patent medicine advertising – was highly significant in promoting what he calls a 'therapeutic ethos'. By offering a relationship with commodities, this form of advertising address promised to alleviate the perceived stresses of contemporary life and to bolster individuals' sense of autonomy which was thought to be compromised by the 'iron cage of bureaucratic "rationality". . . . The therapeutic ethos promised to heal the wounds inflicted by rationalization, to release the cramped energies of a fretful bourgeoisie' (Lears 1983: 17). Lears' formulation of a therapeutic ethos emphasizes one way in which bio-politics fostered and utilized a form of connection between the human body and the commodity. Channelling ways of conceiving bodies and attempting to direct consumption practices, advertising offered potential for controlling the social body through regulating consumption. Foucault argues that during the nineteenth century, visualizing practices shifted such that 'illness, counter-nature, death, in short, the whole dark underside of disease came to light, at the same time illuminating and eliminating itself like night, in the deep, visible, solid, enclosed, but accessible space of the human body' (Foucault 2000a: 195). This was a reorganization of disease in which 'the limits of the visible and the invisible follow a new pattern' (ibid.).

I suggest that these new patterns of the visible and the space of the human body implicate advertising in their re-mapping of materiality and visuality at the same time as offering new modes of social control for projects of bio-politics. But these complex shifts should not be reduced to a theoretical shorthand positing that culture is becoming 'more visual' or that images are playing a more important role in the social realm (see Chapter 4). These developments are better understood as shifts in the form of relationality between things, persons and the visual. Thus advertising cannot be cast straightforwardly as the prime visual form of the nineteenth century: shifts in visuality occurred on a broader scope than that of traditionally-conceived 'images'. Walter Benjamin, for instance, saw 'the dialectic image' operating through material forms such as the commodity rather than through conventional representational forms like advertising:

> Ambiguity is the figurative appearance of the dialectic, the law of the dialectic at a standstill. This standstill is Utopia, and the dialectical image therefore a dream image. The commodity clearly provides such an image: as fetish. The arcades, which are both house and stars, provide such an image. And such an image is provided by the whore, who is seller and commodity in one.
>
> (Benjamin 1973: 171)

For Benjamin, the dialectical image is not an advertising image; rather, it is the material form that advertising is imagined to represent – the commodity. As a dialectical image, the commodity represents not so much the promise of satisfaction as the troubling relations between things and people: as fetish, the commodity displaces and then conjoins human values and the materiality of the object in new formations. Benjamin underscores this analysis by figuring the prostitute as dialectical image, as epitome of modernity. The prostitute represents the unsettling blurring of boundaries between person and thing in her embodiment of both the salesperson and commodity in one visible form. The formulation of the dialectical image thus stresses the significance of the visual in material forms quite distinct from standard image-forms such as advertisements. Moreover, it offers a cautionary note to those who may wish to cast contemporary mass culture or visual culture as evidence of capitalism's ability to distort reality through techniques of illusionism. Referencing the work of Adorno and Horkheimer (1997 [1944]), Mark Seltzer revisits the critique of illusionism and reconsiders the basis of its long-standing appeal:

> But if the scandalous appeal of illusion has formed the basis of cultural critique from Plato's myth of the cave on, it's not hard to see that such a critique of mass culture amounts to the critique of culture and representation as such. By this view, the real scandal of emergent mass culture at the turn of the century was not so much the compulsive appeal of illusion – the attraction to products 'even though they *see through them*' – but rather the democratization of the privilege

of illusionism or simulation, a privilege antithetical to the very notion of 'the mass' and its obligatory confinement to material needs and its function as a social index of 'the real' and 'choice of necessity'.

(Seltzer 1992: 141, emphasis in original)

According to Seltzer, it is the promise of a redistribution of cultural privilege and particularly the accordance of rights of illusionism to the masses that elicited, and continues to elicit, the most criticism of consumer culture. This was an anxiety on the part of the privileged faced with a democratization of access to the terms of representation and the play of simulation. In the nineteenth century, when the masses had previously functioned as a benchmark of reality and determinant of use-value, they were now being offered entry to a consumer dreamworld of image, imagination and illusion. To supplement Seltzer's account, I would also suggest that the privilege of illusionism included a particular form of access to the terms of person–thing relations. Part of the play of representation – as in the dialectical image – consists of access to the ambiguity of the dialectic and access to the privilege of conceiving connections between persons and commodities. Thus, the pleasures of the department store derived in part from illusionism – the opportunity to manipulate sensory data and imaginative resources – conceiving and reconceiving relationships with commodities and creating new understandings of the self as consumer. This illusionism involves allowing the play of the dialectical image, allowing the swing between animation and objectification embodied in, and constitutive of, commodities and enjoying the fascination engendered by the relationalities of persons and things. It is in this nineteenth-century drama of creation that both commodities and persons (as consumers) were made and remade, and it is primarily women who bore the weight of this symbolism and functioned as representational currency for this creative exchange.

Signs of the times? Gender, commodities and modernity

As I have argued, nineteenth-century commentators viewed women as emblematic of this relationship between things and persons. This was perceived as a dangerous and unstable relationship, finding its ultimate expression in oniomania (shopping mania or compulsive shopping) and kleptomania in which women succumbed to the thrall of commodities. Commodities appeared to act upon the consumer as independent entities, directing behaviour and evacuating the self of will and morality. The expansion of consumer culture was seen as 'engendering a revolution of morals, unleashing egotistic and envious drives among the lower orders and women, which could in turn affect the stability of existing social hierarchies' (Felski 1995: 65). In this context, Foucault's 'dangerous individual' is not merely one who threatens society by violence or theft. The danger represented by female shoppers, oniomaniacs or kleptomaniacs was to the ordering of social hierarchies and the mapping of public space and cultural privilege: these consuming women blurred the boundaries of gender respectability and class distinction which had previously mapped and hierarchized the social field. Thus many contemporary critics have argued that the figure of the consuming woman was 'a semiotically dense site of imaginings of the modern' (Felski 1995: 65). As I noted in the previous section, Walter Benjamin (1973) conceived the figure of the (female) prostitute as dialectical image and cipher of modernity, representing a troubling merging of the commodity-form and the human body. This view represented nineteenth-century understandings of the articulation between the human body and the social body, and highlighted the political stakes implicated in managing the terms of their relationship:

> Above all, Victorian logics of embodiment sought certainty; they found out the way of the world by tautology, ordering culture by ordering the body, ordering the body by discovering in it the germ of social structure. . . . The biological determinism of so much Victorian thinking was thus a means of foreclosing on alternative realities – a way of defining the individual, delimiting the social, and managing the increasingly vexed and confusing relation between the two.
>
> (O'Connor 2000: 14)

Erin O'Connor here points to the conceptual tautologies deployed in nineteenth-century mappings of bodies and social structure. Reading society as a biological entity or human body both defined and drew on understandings which conceived the human body to be structured as a society or in accordance with social norms. Stitching up the fabric of the social and the biological in this way afforded a means of delineating and regulating the articulation of persons and non-persons (such as things). O'Connor's account of the circular Victorian logics of social management through classification provides an apt warning for contemporary commentators who might wish to read figures such as kleptomaniacs or hysterics as literal embodiments of the ills of an age. In one form of such Victorian logics, the social phenomenon of kleptomania represented women's 'natural pathology' – a pathology either of body or mind, triggered variously by the department store or the commodity itself. Whatever the stimulus, it was women's *natural* weakness – read off from her subordinate *social* status – that framed her propensity for pathology. In aiming to critique them, O'Connor (2000) argues, there is a danger of reproducing in contemporary accounts these Victorian tautological relationships between 'social' bodies and 'natural' societies. The result is the collapse of arguments into their subject matter and an impoverished understanding of nineteenth-century discursive patterns. In parallel, Mark Seltzer (1992) argues that many accounts of nineteenth-century society, and indeed of contemporary society, posit women as cultural indicators or litmus tests of the social milieu. This, he suggests, is characterized by 'a tendency to replace an identification of women with the natural with an identification of women with the social' (Seltzer 1992: 127–8). In this discursive backflip, women come to represent – and in some accounts materially *embody* – the social in contrast with their previous taxonomic function as the index of the natural or biological. This produces a, '"realist tautology" – the circular relation between interior states and material conditions . . . that the realist account of the individual as "socially constructed" entails' (ibid.). Drawing on O'Connor's and Seltzer's analyses, it is possible to see how nineteenth-century logics read the body and the social together. These logics produced a hermetically sealed unit in which the social and the biological ratified each other and functioned to manage what were seen as unsettlingly fluid boundaries between persons and things, nature and society. The figure of 'woman' was consistently deployed to stage this encounter and to adjudicate in the relations between persons and commodities in nineteenth-century capitalism. Given this discursive legacy, contemporary accounts that posit women as emblems of modernity or as embodied symbols of the nascent consumer culture should be wary of reproducing those same circular Victorian logics. These saw social structure inscribed in women's bodies, managed those very bodies as a means of ordering society, and policing the boundaries between persons and commodities.

These cautions can help sharpen analyses of commodity relations, the functioning and constitution of gender, and understandings of the articulation of bodies and things. This is a vast and complex field of analysis so, for the purposes of this chapter, I will focus on two related elements. First, nineteenth-century Euro-American societies were concerned about sexual disorder and particularly its manifestation through the developing consumer culture. Felski (1995: 69) argues that kleptomania was perceived as a deviant behaviour that articulated with perceptions both of women and consumerism as it was 'a disease that was codified as both feminine and modern, [and] was a striking instance of the sexual disorder that was seen to lie at the very heart of consumer culture'. This disordering of gender hierarchies manifested itself in many forms, most strikingly in movements for female suffrage and their articulation with consumer culture. Playing on the popular representation of consumer culture as a new site of female pleasures, Suffragists targeted department stores as sites of protest for franchise. On 1 March 1912, the Women's Social and Political Union broke nearly 400 shop windows in central London, causing approximately £5,000 of damage (Rappaport 2000). The aim of the Suffragists, who comprised mainly middle-class women, was to gain press attention for their cause. Their protest was not targeted against consumer culture or the commodification of women, but rather, 'they used public identities and public spaces sanctioned by the new commerce to reshape national politics and the public sphere' (Rappaport 2000: 221). But retailers' and the general public's understandings of the protest were articulated through the gendering of these consumption spaces. It was anxiously noted by police and retailers that, in parallel to the problems of identifying shoplifters, it was difficult to distinguish genuine shoppers from Suffragists intent on damage. A *Daily Telegraph* journalist at the time noted: 'suddenly women who had a moment before appeared to be on peaceful shopping expeditions produced from bags or muffs, hammers, stones and sticks, and began an attack upon the nearest windows' (cited in Rappaport 2000: 215). One Suffragist narrowly escaped arrest by claiming that she was an innocent shopper and merely 'admiring the carpets' (ibid.: 217). Many people were astonished that women would attack the very sites of their newly found pleasures and (limited) freedoms. In a letter to the *Standard* newspaper, Mr Lasenby Liberty of the famous department store challenged Mrs Pankhurst herself 'to state the mental process by which they deem the breaking of the very shrines at which they worship will advance their cause' (ibid.: 215). Thus consumer culture 'allowed suffragists to creatively negotiate the cultural boundaries of politics, physical space, personal identity, and ideology. It gave them a new set of tools for identifying and representing themselves and their needs' (Finnegan 1999: 171). This was a material and explicitly political disordering of gender hierarchies and social structure through claims for enfranchisement.

Second, I suggest that sexual disorder occurred at the level of taxonomy, particularly of gender as type or classification. Foucault's analysis of the new biopolitics of the nineteenth century situated the exercise of power 'at the level of life, the species, the race, the large-scale phenomena of population' (Foucault 1990a: 137). The understanding of the masses as a population was a new taxonomy of people which focused intervention on a new set of variables: 'birth and death rates, life expectancy, fertility, state of heath, frequency of illnesses, patterns of diet and habitation' (Foucault 1990a: 25). But whilst Foucault concerned himself with birth rates and fertility as a key nexus of bio-politics, he bracketed the place of women in his analysis. This inattention to gender obscures the *full* extent to which concepts of type and specification – including gender, but also social class, race and others – were central to nineteenth-century Euro-American societies. New specifications of persons such as 'the dangerous individual' and 'the homosexual' ran parallel, I suggest, to new understandings of gendering processes in bio-politics. Nineteenth-century understandings of gender functioned not only in terms of biological status or social role, but also as a classificatory system which ordered not only sexual differences but the wider structure of the social field. Foucault (1990a: 99) has argued that power is not a *property* of individuals and groups, nor are those groups static units which, once formed, are forever stable; rather, the coalescence of power–knowledge forms groupings that are 'matrices of transformations'. As nodes of power–knowledge, I am suggesting that classifications such as gender and race can be seen as such matrices or taxonomic ordering devices. They are formed by power–knowledge but are also active in reconfiguring modes of classification. In a similar way, Franklin *et al.* argue that gender can function as 'a *productive mechanism or enabling device*' (2000: 7, emphasis in original). In a nineteenth-century context, gender can therefore be understood as a classifying matrix that facilitated, amongst other things, an ordering and hierarchizing of the social world. Women were classified and controlled according to their gender, class and race, but those taxonomies also operated as productive mechanisms to order the social field. Thus, in ways parallel to (but not symmetrical with) other classifications such as race and class, gender functioned as a transformative matrix through which social relations were made and remade, hierarchies constituted and reconstituted. I suggest, therefore, that the sexual disorder which many nineteenth-century and contemporary commentators have considered central to Victorian culture is also a disordering of type or classification. If kleptomania was seen as 'a special form of sex crime' (Spiekermann 1999: 149), it was also a crime against nineteenth-century taxonomic structures. It was a crime committed by women but was not thought to be unambiguously rooted in women's physiology. As I have argued, the attributed causes of consuming disorders shifted in nineteenth-century discourses between women's bodies, the site of the department store, the material appeal of the commodity-form itself, and an individual weakness of will or morality. Viewed as an unhealthy relation between (and even mingling of) person and commodity, kleptomania and oniomania were boundary infringements of type and classification. Women and their role in kleptomania and other consuming practices functioned as taxonomic benchmarks that offered to Victorian societies epistemological certainty and ideals of social order. Thus, women's symbolic role was not restricted to that of an emblem of the social: gender operated as part of a classificatory regime that regulated social structure. Forms of 'dangerous consumption' such as klepto-mania or consuming alcohol to the point of 'addiction', represented taxonomic breakdown and a disordering of the relations between things and persons, com-modities and consumers. Hence Benjamin's (1973) view of the (female) prostitute as an emblem of modernity – embodying both the person and a commodity – can be expanded: the discursive figuring of the prostitute was also an expression of anxieties about classificatory disorders in the relations between persons and things, and represented an underlying concern about the new culture of commodities.

Attempts to realign such disruptions in the authorized declension of persons, of things, and the strictly policed relations between them took many forms. As I have noted, the upper and middle classes drew on their material privilege to construct collections of objects. In tabulating or ordering those objects, Victorians sought to control the social order (and its relation to the natural) through systems of analogy. Alongside this focus on objects, people figured prominently in this regulatory schema which is nowhere more evident than in the practices of, and debates around, slavery (see Kopytoff 1986; Sheller 2000, 2003). Here, persons were treated as things, or more precisely, as property which could be bought and sold. Slavery can therefore be seen as a violent management of the classifications of 'person' and 'thing' for commercial and political gain. As Kopytoff (1986: 64) suggests, this boundary control of the socially determined categories of person and thing should not be considered an ahistorical concern: 'the conceptual polarity of individualized persons and commoditized things is recent and, culturally speaking, exceptional'. Its multiple forms can be tracked through the diversity of social, political and economic orderings of societies. But this chapter has not attempted such a scale of analysis, offering instead a synthesis of accounts of nineteenth-century Euro-American cultures which emphasizes the specificity of relations between commodities, persons and advertisements. Foucault (1990a) has argued that one specificity of this place and time was the development of bio-power, a form of control that was indispensable to the development of capitalism. Linked to new ways of conceiving society through statistics (see Hacking 1990), 'the growth of a capitalist economy gave rise to the specific modality of disciplinary power, whose general formulas, techniques of submitting forces and bodies, in short, "political anatomy", could be operated in the most diverse political régimes, apparatuses or institutions' (Foucault 1991: 221). The new modes of control afforded by bio-politics constituted the masses as a population and submitted this population to regulatory regimes centred around reproduction and health, and also around new classifications of race and singularized identities such as the 'dangerous individual'.

But I have suggested that the development of these modalities of power also facilitated a new mapping of the political anatomy of *things* and their relations to persons. This 'politics of synthetics' as I have called it, is a form of control over singularized bodies and massed people, but also over but the conceptual benchmarks of type, genre and classification.

This chapter has explored how understandings of consumer culture and of consuming disorders such as kleptomania and 'alcohol addiction' emerged in an interwoven form in the nineteenth century. These articulations were key in defining concepts of freedom, will, and the distinction between need and want in a culture of consumption. Figuring deviant consuming practices or pathologies such as kleptomania provided Victorians with a way of exploring their social norms and constituting new norms through consumption. In particular, it afforded a means of rehearsing a pressing nineteenth-century concern, that is, the terms of what it meant to be human and what it meant to be animate. This was frequently articulated in the perceived relations of persons to things – especially commodities – that had come to be seen as 'strangely-animated objects' acting independently of persons (Camhi 1993: 34). Thus, the new framing of consuming practices through notions of addiction, compulsion and pathology formed a key nexus for the elaboration of the relations between things and persons, and functioned as for important sites for policing boundary infringements. The causes of these consuming disorders were not attributed to advertisements; the causes were unsystematically distributed between commodity or substance itself, site or location (such as the department store), weakness of will or moral debility, and biological propensity. In contrast, as I argue in later chapters, many of today's 'consuming disorders' – such as excessive use of credit cards or practices of 'compulsive shopping' – are thought to be channelled through (or even directly caused by) advertising, the corollary of which is ever-stricter regulation for advertising 'dangerous commodities' such as tobacco.[2] Nineteenth-century advertising functioned in a different social context with a different form of relationality between things and persons, commodities and consumers. But whilst advertising was not thought to manipulate individuals or direct 'pathological' consumption practices in the nineteenth century, there are certain important parallels with the contemporary functions of advertising and definitions of deviant consumption. Nineteenth-century 'pathological' consumption practices, alongside categories of gender, operated as classificatory devices or taxonomic tools which managed modes of specification. This function is most strikingly evident in the distinctions made and reinforced between persons and things, consumers and commodities. The challenge presented by the nascent commodity culture to those established taxonomic boundaries channelled under-standings of a loss of agency, and a loss of humanity as the perceived power of the material world grew: the world of things, of commodities, was thought to be encroaching on the world of the human and leeching away that very essence of human existence. As I argue in the following chapters, contemporary advertising operates in a manner analogous to, but more subtle in comparison to, those nineteenth-century conceptions: it orders and reorders social classifications and, more particularly, the conceptual distinctions between humans and the material world, between persons and things. In the next chapter, I explore how contemporary regulatory debates and practices frame advertising and how they attempt to redress the balance of power against the perceived lure of the commodity and the intensity of the material world.

2 Advertising as site of contestation

Criticisms, controversy and regulation

This chapter focuses on contemporary consuming controversies and explores the way in which advertising functions as a lightning rod, channelling a range of social, political and economic concerns. In earthing these currents of critical intervention, advertising in the twentieth and twenty-first centuries has been consistently subjected to intense criticism and has been cast as primary mediator of social degeneration, moral debasement and a range of other retrograde social shifts. Taking as a case study the regulation of advertising for 'dangerous commodities', this analysis is situated precisely during the dying days of tobacco advertising – a ban on such advertising came into force in the UK on 14 February 2003 and, at the time of writing, a European Union directive banning print advertisements has been agreed. In addition, the World Health Organization's Framework Convention on Tobacco Control, that imposes global restrictions on tobacco advertising, was agreed in May 2003. I offer an analysis of a particular moment and the cultural concerns and political imperatives that it condenses. But the scope of my analysis is not limited to advertising for 'dangerous commodities' such as tobacco and alcohol: a key part of my argument is that regulatory practices (and commercial practices aimed at deflecting criticism and regulation) actively expand the definition of 'dangerous advertising' such that all advertising comes to be seen as threatening or framed as a social pathogen. Nor is my analysis restricted to the specific debates circulating during this intense period of regulatory concern; this chapter tracks how regulatory regimes form one element of the 'circuits of belief' in and about advertising that constitute an important, on-going form of relationality between commodities and advertisements, persons and images. To explore this circulation of perceptions about advertising, and the relations between advertising images and commodities, I examine the ways in which the following important groups figure the power or effects of advertising: (1) regulatory bodies such as the Advertising Standards Authority; (2) the advertising trade associations of the Institute for Practitioners in Advertising and the Advertising Association, and non-governmental organizations such as the World Health Organization; and (3) UK and European Union (EU) directives on advertising. In Chapter 3, I expand this analysis to encompass advertising agencies and the personal and commercial investments of advertising practitioners in these circuits of belief. Regulatory bodies, trade associations and non-governmental organizations discursively construct advertising for particular commercial or social purposes. In parallel to UK and EU legislation, these groups aim to license their claims by drawing on widely circulating perceptions of advertising as well as diverse forms of research.

My interest lies in analysing the form of relationality or type of connection between discourses circulating within and amongst advertising regulatory bodies, trade associations, legislation and academic analyses. As Foucault (2001: 49) has argued, discourses are not merely the intersection of words and things, nor 'groups of signs (signifying elements referring to contents or representations)'; instead, discourses are 'practices that systematically form the objects of which they speak'. Hence, beliefs in and about advertising that circulate in the discursive practices of these distinct groups generate material effects, stabilizing and materializing the cultural and economic form that we know as advertising. In my analysis, I focus on the 'enunciative modalities' (Foucault 2001: 50) in the circuits of belief: who is licensed to generate discourse about advertising? What is the institutional site from which those discourses are produced? What is the positioning of the subjects of authority – as speaking, as listening, as observing? In this way I analyse the 'procedures of intervention' (Foucault 2001: 58) into the constitution of advertising as a cultural and economic form. This focus on intervention foregrounds the issue of regulation but, as I demonstrate in the next chapter, it also encompasses the ways in which advertising agencies intervene in the circulation of beliefs in advertising and flow of legitimacy between different authorities of knowledge about advertising. The issue of regulation thus crystallizes cultural concerns at any given moment and offers a useful point of analytic access to the formation that is advertising. As I demonstrated in Chapter 1, sites and substances of controversy shift in relation to historical and cultural contexts. In this chapter, I focus on tobacco and alcohol advertising as an important contemporary site of contention that channels current concerns about advertising and about 'dangerous commodities'. But in this analysis I am not attempting to uncover the 'truths' of advertising which some might locate in the practices and discourses of agencies or regulatory bodies. Indeed, my analysis suggests that the truths of advertising practices, effects and discourses are provisionally interwoven to form a complex promotional nexus. Nor do I aim to expose the 'truths' of advertising texts using textual analysis or semiotic 'power tools'. In Chapter 4, I argue that examining the textuality of advertisements as a genre and their form of relationality to things and persons is a more productive approach than a conventional textual analysis of specific advertisements. This chapter, then, aims to track the circulation of beliefs in and about advertising in ways that do justice to their complex connections and disconnections whilst attempting to avoid the blunt foreshortening typical of many understandings of advertising.

Regulating culture

Whilst there is a general awareness today of the ubiquity of advertising in the nineteenth century, there remains a powerful sense of advertising as a thoroughly contemporary form. Partly due to its constant promotion of novelty, advertising is imagined to be the sign of the times, representing the leading edge of social change. It is this perception of advertising's role in stimulating or channelling social change – and particularly social degeneration – that contributes to the volume of criticism that is directed at advertising from the media, politicians, academics, anti-consumerist pressure groups and the general public. As I argue in the final section of this chapter, this perception is partially due to advertising's commercial imperative to present itself as a key driver of cultural change even if many advertising practitioners do not characterise their role or the impact of their advertisements in this way.

The perception that advertising is a relatively new cultural form that has only recently attracted criticism and regulation is inaccurate. As early as the mid-seventeenth century, there were attacks on the promotion of goods, especially 'quack cures' by 'Charlatans' (Elliott 1962: 102). In eighteenth-, nineteenth- and early twentieth-century Britain, criticism of advertising existed in many forms. For instance, the National Society for Controlling Abuses of Public Advertising (SCAPA) was set up at end of the nineteenth century (Nevett 1982). This was a minority pressure group run by the upper and middle classes and focused its criticism on advertising signs and hoardings.

> Through campaigns in the press and through their publication, *A Beautiful World*, members of the society sought 'to protect the picturesque simplicity of rural and river scenery and to promote due regard to the dignity and propriety of aspect in towns', and 'to assert generally the national importance of maintaining the elements of interest and beauty of out-of-doors life'.
>
> (Fraser 1981: 137)

SCAPA exerted considerable pressure and, following the controversial projection of magic lantern advertisements onto Nelson's column and the National Gallery in London, influenced the passing of an 1894 bill restricting advertisements (Fraser 1981). The society also influenced the 1907 Advertisements Regulation Act that 'empowered local authorities to make bye-laws for the regulation of hoardings and the protection of certain amenities' (Nevett 1982: 118). By the end of 1914, thirty counties and thirty-four boroughs had made bye-laws under the act. Yet the criticisms levelled at advertising by SCAPA and other individuals did not focus primarily on 'false claims' in advertising or its manipulative powers. Rather, the criticism was aesthetic in nature, lamenting the proliferation of advertisements and their consequent aesthetic pollution of public (urban and rural) space. In that period, criticism of advertising was very much a middle and upper class preoccupation, but the form that such criticism took was multiple: sandwich-board men were targeted for inappropriately wearing military uniform; advertisers were upbraided for printing fake banknotes and coins as gimmicks and for sending advertising telegrams, which in 1914 were known popularly as notices of relatives' death at war (Nevett 1982). The criticisms of advertising shifted and acquired a different currency as the century progressed. By the 1920s, criticisms of advertising were beginning to take the form of those circulating today. Here, Jeremy Tunstall cites

Sir Charles Higham's 1925 remarks summarizing criticisms of advertising; 'It is said: (1) that the cost of advertising is so extravagant that it creates fictitious prices, (2) that advertising is so persuasive that it can sell dishonest goods, and (3) that it generates artificial demands' (cited in Tunstall 1964: 236). As these 1925 criticisms have since become almost axiomatic approaches to advertising that operate across political, popular and academic registers, it has become difficult to recognize that criticisms of advertising are historically specific. Such criticisms derive not from any essence of advertising's form or function, but from particular historically-situated social concerns and understandings of advertising's impact.

Parallel to understandings of advertising as a prototypical form of the twentieth or twenty-first century, there is a general perception that nineteenth-century advertising was a largely unregulated business that was only later subjected to sustained censure. Contrary to this assumption, advertising in Britain was subjected to various forms of legislation throughout the nineteenth century. For instance, obscene advertisements were targeted using the 1824 Vagrancy Act, street advertisers (hoardings etc.) were restricted by the Metropolitan Paving Act of 1817, and the 1839 Metropolitan Police Act allowed for a general control of advertising (Nevett 1982). Omnibus and sandwich board men were restricted by the London Hackney Carriage Act of 1853, and the 1889 Indecent Advertisements Act was aimed at curbing medical/quack advertisements that often featured references to sexually transmitted diseases (ibid.). Self-regulation also existed as newspapers and advertisers operated informal self-censorship in order to filter out certain advertisements, especially on the grounds of truthfulness. The first formalized self-regulatory system was set up in 1890 when the United Bill-Posters Association and the London Bill-Posters Association set up a Joint Censorship Committee that was designed to exclude the obscene, the offensive or the overly-sensational. In the early twentieth century, the advertising industry as a body starting taking formal responsibility for its products when the Advertising Association set up a National Vigilance Committee (ibid.). In America at the same period, trade associations and publishers were attempting to create an image of professionalism and respectability for advertising by promoting standards of commercial behaviour (Pease 1958). By the 1930s, American trade associations were making considerable efforts to stave off external regulation and 'seemed more concerned with persuading others that internal regulation was strict and effective than they were with actually making it so' (Pease 1958: 73). This industry-driven imperative to demonstrate social responsibility developed throughout the twentieth century in response to potential threats to the industry's autonomy. As controversies around advertising for specific commodities such as tobacco grew, and as the threat of government regulation of advertising intensified, the advertising industry searched for ways of demonstrating its social and commercial responsibility. In the mid-1950s, advertising became the focus of critiques fuelled by Vance Packard's now infamous 1957 book, *The Hidden Persuaders*, in which Packard accused advertising of developing sinister new techniques of psychological manipulation. According to Packard, the most frighteningly effective of these techniques was subliminal advertising that supposedly infiltrated individuals with commercial messages below the level of consciousness. At the height of this controversy, the Institute for Practitioners in Advertising in the UK took the initiative to demonstrate the industry's responsible self-regulation by declaring subliminal advertising to be 'professionally unacceptable' (Turner 1965: 288). The controversy channelled widespread popular fears about the invasive powers of advertising into the idea of subliminal advertising, and in condemning it, the IPA blew the issue up into 'an absurd bogey' (ibid.). There was no evidence to suggest that agencies were engaging in subliminal advertising, nor even that such a technique was possible. But the IPA succeeded in promoting an image of the industry as efficiently self-regulating and temporarily managed to deflect attention – and the threat of statutory regulation – away from the sensitive issues of tobacco and alcohol advertising and advertising to children (Brierley 1995). By tapping into and recirculating certain unsubstantiated but highly discursively charged beliefs about advertising, the industry attempted to ground its status as a responsible profession and restate the legitimacy of self-regulation. Therefore, the significance of the controversy about subliminal advertising did not reside in its supposed effects or even in the possibility of its very existence; rather, it lay in how it became a trope for defences, critiques and conspiracy theories about the powers of advertising. As one advertising practitioner is quoted as saying, subliminal advertising became the 'UFO of business' (Leiss *et al.* 1990: 371).

Further pre-emptive moves by the UK advertising industry were to follow. An independent body called the Advertising Inquiry Committee was established in 1959 to monitor 'all kinds of harmful advertising' (Nevett 1982: 198). In 1961, the Advertising Association unveiled the British Code of Advertising Practice that was the first set of formal standards for all elements of the advertising business. This move towards more formalized self-regulation was a response to increasing pressure from various consumer and environmental groups. In 1962, the Advertising Standards Authority was set up in order to provide independent scrutiny of the newly created self-regulatory system (ASA 2000e).[1] This drive for self-regulation spread across Europe culminating in the establishment of the European Advertising Tripartite in 1980. This was an active partner of the European Association of Advertising Agencies that had been founded in Oslo in 1959. One of the main functions of the EAAA has been to lobby governments and the EU against the option of statutory regulation by extolling the efficiency of industry self-regulation (Mattelart 1991). Another body, the European Advertising Standards Alliance (EASA), similarly functions to promote the role of industry self-regulation and was active in attempting to derail statutory legislation on advertising proposed in the EU Tobacco Advertising Directive 2001/0119. In the USA, similar moves to divert pressure for external regulation occurred. For instance, in 1971 the Association of National Advertisers, the American Association of Advertising Agencies, the American Advertising Federation and the Council for Better Business Bureaus introduced a new system to regulate deception in advertising (Pope 1983).

Yet statutory regulation of advertising may not address the concerns of such regulatory moves: such regulation can have unforeseen, and sometimes positive, consequences for the advertising industry and their clients. For instance, the US ban on broadcast advertisements for cigarettes that came into force on 1 January 1971 demonstrates the complexity of the social and economic issues at stake. The then Chairman of the Federal Trade Commission believed that the ban on broadcast cigarette advertising may actually have been beneficial for the tobacco industry. As Schudson (1993: 99) notes, 'television advertising was increasingly expensive and the anti-smoking commercials were having some effect. Moreover, the visibility of television advertising, while perhaps a commercial asset, was a serious political liability'. Moreover, the commercial effects were not straightforwardly negative. Spending on magazine and newspaper advertising increased 145 per cent in 1971, whilst total tobacco industry spending on advertising dropped by 20 per cent (Craig and Moellinger 2001). This represented a streamlining of expenditure coupled with more efficient targeting of consumers: the new focus on magazine advertising enabled the industry to target specific audiences more precisely and in a more cost-effective way. In addition, 'the ban decreased competition in the industry, limited the entry of new brands, and overall, increased tobacco company profit margins' (Craig and Moellinger 2001: 66). So whilst there is considerable pressure today to regulate advertising – pressure that has resulted in an outright ban of tobacco advertising in the UK – the commercial effects of such regulatory moves remain ambiguous.

To examine the detail of contemporary advertising regulation and the forces that motivate it, I will focus on the Advertising Standards Authority and the Independent Television Commission in the UK. The USA has a two-tier self-regulatory system established by the advertising industry in 1971 that consists of the National Advertising Division of the Council for Better Business Bureaus (NAD) and the National Advertising Review Body (NARB). NAD is the investigative body, whilst NARB is the appeals body of the system. I am restricting my analysis primarily to British regulatory processes with a complementary analysis of British advertising agencies in the next chapter, yet the insights I draw from this approach offer important avenues of analysis for American and other European processes. As I have argued, criticism and regulatory control of advertising is not new. My aim in this section is to analyse the particular constellation of concerns and perceptions that constitute contemporary understandings of advertising: how do these organizations figure the role and effects of advertising in the way they produce and institute the regulatory codes? In what way do these institutions intervene in the circuits of belief in and about advertising?

As noted above, the Advertising Standards Authority (ASA) was established in the UK in 1962 to implement and monitor the self-regulatory system that had been instituted by the advertising industry. As an industry-funded organization, its function is to deflect drives for increased regulation and to promote the industry's interests; for instance, it staunchly defended industry self-regulation in the face of challenges presented by the draft of the new Communications Bill in the UK that proposed a radical overhaul of media organization. Funded by a surcharge placed on advertising display and direct marketing expenditure, the ASA's remit covers advertisements in newspapers, magazines, brochures, leaflets, circulars, mailings, fax transmissions, catalogues, follow-up literature and other electronic and printed material, posters, cinema and video commercials, non-broadcast electronic material, and sales promotions. As broadcast advertising for cigarettes has been banned in the UK since 1965, the main form tobacco advertising has taken until its ban in 2003 has been print and poster advertising which is monitored by the ASA. The ASA only assesses advertisements against which a complaint has been made and which fall within the scope of The British Codes of Advertising and Sales. These are a detailed set of benchmarks for appropriate advertising content and style and are drawn up by the Committee of Advertising Practice (CAP) which is constituted by representatives from the industry, government bodies and trade associations including the Advertising Association and the Institute of Practitioners in Advertising. The Codes 'do not have force of law and their interpretation will reflect their flexibility'; in effect, the ASA operates a non-statutory, self-regulatory system. The sanctions available to the ASA are as follows: 'the media, contractors and service providers may withhold their services or deny access to space; adverse publicity, which acts as a deterrent, may result from rulings published in the ASA's Monthly Report; pre-vetting or trading sanctions may be imposed or recognition revoked by the media's, advertiser's, promoter's or agency's professional association' (ASA 2000a: Code 68.39).

The UK's Independent Television Commission (ITC) derives its powers from the Broadcasting Acts of 1990 and 1996. Unlike the ASA Codes, the ITC Codes have statutory status and were the framework for the ban on tobacco advertising on television until 2003 when the Tobacco Advertising and Promotion Act took over their role. The ITC publishes its Codes and guidelines for broadcast advertising, and distributes licences for commercial television companies to broadcast in and from the UK. Its remit is not restricted to advertising, and includes the monitoring of programme content, sponsorship and technical performance. Unlike the ASA, the ITC can impose financial penalties on broadcasters and, in extreme cases, can effect 'the curtailment and eventual rescinding of a broadcaster's licence' (Independent Television Commission 1998). It also publishes the ITC Code of Advertising Standards and Practice that mirrors the ASA Codes and aims to ensure that broadcast advertising 'is not misleading; does not encourage or condone harmful behaviour; does not cause widespread or exceptional offence' (ITC 1998: 4).[2] However, the ITC does not preview advertisements and only considers them after they have been broadcast. In order to address this anomaly, the broadcasters set up and continue to fund the Broadcast Advertising Clearance Centre (BACC) whose function is to advise them on the legal requirements for advertisements they wish to broadcast. BACC views every broadcast commercial before it is aired and provides its own Notes of Guidance which supplement the ITC Codes. Whilst the ITC may override BACC pre-transmission clearance, this occurs only very rarely. Equally, most agencies, clients and broadcasters abide by BACC decisions with only a few exceptions. One example is a Miller Pilsner beer commercial that had been refused BACC clearance but Channels 4 and 5 decided to air it after 11 p.m. despite this. Complaints were then made to the ITC for unacceptable language and the ITC required that the advertisement be removed.

Both the ASA and ITC affirm that the key principle of the Codes is that 'all advertisements should be legal, decent, honest and truthful' and that 'no advertisement should bring advertising into disrepute'. The two bodies both demonstrate clear concern for the profile of advertising and the potential damage to commercial interests that may occur should advertising's image become further tarnished. The BACC Notes of Guidance state that, 'unless television advertising is consistently honest and truthful – and unless it is seen to be so – it will lose public confidence and its power to persuade will diminish' (Broadcast Advertising Clearance Centre 1999: Paragraph 1.1.1). At the same time, the ASA states that, 'the rules make due allowance for public sensitivities but will not be used by the ASA to diminish freedom of speech'. In this case, advertising is defined as commercial free speech that must be protected. In fact, the ASA frames its self-regulation as clearly beneficial to commercial concerns:

> The strength of the system depends on the long-term commitment of all those involved in commercial communications. Practitioners in every sphere share an interest in seeing that advertisements and promotions are welcomed and trusted by their audience; unless they are accepted and believed they cannot succeed. If they are offensive or misleading they discredit everyone associated with them and the industry as a whole.
>
> (ASA 2000a: Code 68.2)

This concern with advertising's image is expressed in the Codes in a range of ways. Upholding standards of taste and decency is one theme that emerges strongly from both the ASA and ITC Codes: 'No advertisement may offend against good taste or decency or be offensive to public feeling and no advertisement should prejudice respect for human dignity' (ITC 1998: point 13). Both bodies base their rulings on imagined contemporary mores. As Claire Forbes, Head of Communications at the ASA, told me in an interview, 'what [the council of the ASA] are always trying to do, particularly in cases of taste and decency, is to reflect what they perceive the British public to feel'. Whilst the ASA engages in various research projects to gauge public sensibilities, for example on the use of strong language in advertisements, the final decision as to the benchmarks for taste and decency is clearly a matter of interpretation and judgement. This is played out in the adjudications of the ASA. For example, a complaint against a Boddington's beer press advertisement on the basis of offence at the language used, and at an oblique reference to cannabis use, was not upheld by the ASA. The ASA appeared to accept the agency's plea that they 'had not intended to offend'.

But whilst issues of taste and decency attract considerable media attention – usually focusing on nudity or strong language – other forms of complaints are more prevalent. In 2001, only 20 per cent of complaints made to the ASA were about taste and decency (ASA 2001a). As Forbes states, 'one of the things that we found in [ASA] research was that the general public is very concerned about misleading advertising . . . but it's the taste and decency issues that always get the press attention'. So despite the considerable media attention directed at advertisements deemed controversial, it is important to recognize that the overall number of complaints about advertisements is relatively small. The single advertisement that generated the most complaints in the ASA's history was a British Safety Council leaflet promoting condom use and featuring an image of the Pope and the text, 'Eleventh Commandment: "Thou shalt always wear a condom"'. The advertisement received only 1,187 complaints. In 2001, the ASA received 12,600 complaints relating to 9,945 advertisements in the context of an estimated 30 million press advertisements published in the UK in one year and, of those complaints, 6.5 per cent were deemed to have breached the codes (ASA 2001a). Many complaints to both the ASA and ITC focus on the misleading nature of advertisements, particularly with reference to advertisements targeted at children. The ITC Codes state that no advertising should take advantage of 'children's natural credulity' and calls on advertisers to take account of the fact that 'children's ability to distinguish between fact and fantasy will vary according to their age and individual personality' (ITC 1998: Appendix 1). The BACC Codes also place a strong emphasis on keeping advertisements distinct from programmes and programme trailers (BACC 1999: Code 2.3.1). This concern about the potentially misleading elements of advertise-ments is played out in complaints to regulatory bodies and is inscribed in the bodies' own Codes in terms of a problematic and unstable relationship between fiction and reality. Quite apart from any advertisement that straightforwardly misleads or makes false claims about a product or service, the distinction in the Codes between fiction and reality places advertising firmly on the side of fiction and falsehood, and television programmes on the side of reality. This paradoxical distinction appears to gain its discursive force from the *commercial* status of advertising. This perception belies the fact that much television is itself commercial and partly funded by advertising. In addition, television programmes – even documentary or news programmes – clearly draw on televisual conventions and selective editing processes that problematize their status as 'reality'. Despite these anomalies, advertising is relegated to the realm of falsehood primarily through its status as commercial persuasion. Moreover, the emphasis on demonstrating the reality of a product is unevenly applied, particularly when 'dangerous commodities' are at issue. One ITC Code on the portrayal of alcohol's properties or effects states that, 'advertisements must not claim that alcohol has therapeutic qualities nor offer it as a stimulant, sedative or tranquilliser' (ITC 1998: Code 40[d]). Here, the presentation of what are seen as 'realities' of alcohol's properties is censored rather than defended in the Codes. The 'reality' of alcohol and alcohol advertisements is instead aligned with the imagined effects of advertising, namely that advertising success-fully persuades its viewers to consume that product.

Unlike most nineteenth-century criticisms, it is this issue of effects that lies at the heart of criticisms levelled at advertising by politicians, the general public, pressure groups, and many academics. It also takes a central place in regulatory codes, but in an uneasy and ill-defined manner. For instance, ITC Codes state that, 'advertise-ments must not foster, depict or imply immoderate drinking' (ITC 1998: Code 40 [l]), yet the Codes do not make clear how an advertisement might 'foster' behaviour or how such an advertisement could be identified. In parallel, the ASA Codes state that advertisements should contain nothing 'that is likely to lead people to adopt styles of drinking that are unwise' and they should not encourage 'excessive drinking' (ASA 2000a: Codes 46.2, 46.3). 'No advertisement should incite people to start smoking' and 'advertisements should not encourage smokers to increase their consumption or smoke to excess' (ASA 2000a: Codes 66.13, 66.14). Whilst the Codes nowhere clarify how to recognize an advertisement engaged in these persuasive practices, there is a detailed set of Codes outlining with great precision unacceptable representational approaches in advertisements: people shown drinking alcohol should not be or appear to be under twenty-five years old; smoking should not be associated with social or sexual success; cigarette advertisements 'should avoid any suggestion of a healthy or wholesome style of life' (ASA 2000a: Code 66.25); advertisements 'should not suggest that any alcoholic drink can enhance mental, physical or sexual capabilities, popularity, attractiveness, masculinity, femininity or sporting achievements' (ASA 2000a: Code 46.7). These Codes are implemented in the regulatory bodies' adjudications in ways which highlight the difficulties in gauging the effects of advertising. For example, a complaint made to the ITC against a Miller Genuine Draft beer broadcast advertisement that features cars stationary in a traffic jam and people drinking the beer, argued that the advertisement encouraged drink-driving. The complaint was not upheld as the ITC 'did not believe that the advertisement would in fact encourage drink-driving' (ITC 2001: 5). Yet no account was given by the ITC of why they believed this or how they reached their decision. This lack of detail is also evident in adjudications for complaints that are upheld. Complaints were made in 2000 to the ASA about press and poster advertisements for First Quench, a mail order alcoholic drinks service. The advertisement featured a smiling man saying, 'It was the best thing about my birthday . . . 6 beers before midday' (ASA 2000c: 1). One complaint from the pressure group Alcohol Concern argued that the advertisement encouraged excessive drinking. The ASA upheld the complaint and in its adjudication stated that 'readers could infer from the headline that the character had drunk six beers before midday and within a fairly limited time period. . . . The advertisement . . . could encourage excessive drinking' (ibid.). Again, the adjudication does not detail precisely how an advertisement might impact upon behaviour and assumes a straightforwardly mimetic relation between representation and consumption practices. Indeed, the adjudications draw on 'commonsense' views of the perceived effects of advertising on behaviour. This mirroring of general perceptions of advertising in the discourses of the ASA and ITC is set alongside the way in which their adjudications come to mirror the cryptic, ironic tone of much contemporary advertising for cigarettes and alcohol. In one complaint against a poster advertisement for Smirnoff vodka with the headline, '. . . If Smirnoff made pain killers', the ASA adjudication describes the offending advertisement in some detail. In doing so, the adjudication reproduces the same surreal tone as the advertising text itself:

> The advertisers said the poster was intended to be so surreal and humorous that members of the public would find it incredible. They believed a naked man sliding down a banister towards a finial was so extreme that no one would be incited to drink excessively and copy that behaviour. Although

it acknowledged that it was intended to be humorous, the Authority considered that the poster depicted drunken activity and could encourage excessive drinking.

(ASA 2000b: 1)

The adjudication goes on to discuss exhaustively, and with considerable straight-faced pedantry, whether the character would be perceived by the public to be naked or wearing flesh-coloured underwear. Here, the adjudication becomes as surreal a text as the advertisement itself and the issue of impact upon behaviour becomes displaced by an elaborate discussion of representational detail.

As I have argued above, the regulatory codes of advertising in the UK function through a general belief that advertising 'works' (that it directs consumption behaviour) and therefore requires regulation. Yet the detail of the Codes reveal inherent ambiguities and difficulties in defining precise effects. The Codes for the most controversial commodities such as tobacco and alcohol make no specific reference to addiction, habit or dependency. Instead, they target advertisements that are considered to foster 'excessive', 'unwise' or 'immoderate' drinking or smoking, yet they have no benchmarks for making such judgements. In the absence of sound criteria for assessing the extent to which an advertisement might encourage excessive consumption, it is the representational practice itself that takes the brunt of the regulation. In one complaint against a poster advertisement for Red Square alcoholic drink, the ASA (2000d: 1) adjudication describes the offending advertisement in some detail:

[The ASA] noted the headline stated 'Sleep when you're dead' and the scene, which featured a low sun and an empty road, suggested that it had been photographed at dawn, both factors that implied the featured people, who seemed euphoric, had been drinking all night. The Authority concluded that the poster irresponsibly condoned and encouraged excessive drinking.

In a tone of a detective novel, the ASA painstakingly describes the scene of the crime, motive and culprit. The proof is provided in the detailed reproduction of the representation not in any discussion of the mechanisms of how an advertisement might affect individual behaviour. The regulatory practices of the ASA come to focus on patterns of representational practice rather than on patterns of consumption per se. It is the general *practice of advertising* that comes to be critiqued and pathologized rather than the commodity itself, the act of consumption, or even any particular advertisement. An analysis of the 'enunciative modalities' (Foucault 2001: 50) of the regulatory bodies thus reveals a pattern of textual description: in detailing the textual form of the advertisements, regulators intervene in the circuits of belief about advertising by mapping, and hence circumscribing and constituting, the cultural and economic form that is advertising.

Hence, in an intriguing shift of emphasis, it is *advertising itself* rather than any 'dangerous commodities' that comes to define 'excess', 'the immoderate', 'the unwise' and particularly the unhealthy: it is a pathologization of the representational form. Of course, this chimes well with the generally circulating perception that advertising is 'too much'. The imagined excesses of advertising, which have long-established currency, are now put to work in an attempt to define the field of consumption and what should be subject to regulation: advertising is too powerful; too manipulative; too commodified; too pervasive; too commercial. The regulatory bodies have arrived at such a position due to the tensions in attempting to regulate advertising in an era in which consumption represents the ultimate individual experience of freedom. The ASA, which operates self-regulatory codes unlike the statutory codes of the ITC, needs to be seen to be monitoring advertising effectively whilst also defending the interests of the advertising industry to advertise as freely as possible. The ASA is funded by an industry levy on advertising and was set up specifically to forestall full statutory regulation of advertising. Together with the complexities of monitoring advertising's effects, this puts the ASA in an ambiguous position. For instance, in January 2000 – before the ban on tobacco advertising was in place – the Society of Cardiothoracic Surgeons complained about a Henri Wintermans press advertisement for Cafe Creme Fresco cigars (ASA 2000f: 1). They claimed that the advertisement explicitly targeted women and that this was particularly irresponsible in the light of the rising incidence of lung cancer in women. The ASA did not uphold this complaint, accepting the advertiser's claims that the campaign was not targeting a specific gender and was not aimed at encouraging people to start smoking; rather, it was intended to encourage established smokers to switch brands. The ASA also argued that 'if smoking was classified as an unsafe practice all tobacco advertising would breach the Codes'. This statement sums up the ironies and contradictions of advertising regulation. Clearly, smoking has been recognized by the medical establishment and public opinion for many years as an unsafe practice. Yet the ASA Codes themselves do not refer to addiction, habit or dependency, and health issues are referenced only obliquely in terms of 'unwise' or 'excessive' smoking or drinking practices. The Codes therefore operate as a textual zero-sum game: they present a detailed set of strictures whose coherence is only guaranteed by displacing issues of advertising effects and the effects of consuming commodities such as tobacco onto the text of the advertisement. This does not jar with general perceptions of advertising that tend to locate the imagined powers of advertising in its textual sophistry. ASA adjudications are thus based on an arbitrary representational scrutiny, the scope of which is defined by the text of the Codes, in which a detailing of the imagistic, textual qualities of an advertisement provides the grounding for judgement. This circular arithmetic of textuality draws on circuits of belief about advertising and effectively elides issues of material effects whilst giving the appearance of a rigorous and efficient self-regulatory procedure. Whilst this analysis is based on advertisements for commodities such as tobacco and alcohol I am suggesting that, by a process of contagion, such understandings of advertising expand to encompass all its forms.

But my claim must be nuanced: it is not accurate to say that regulatory bodies create false representations of advertising and its effects. They generate, circulate, and are fuelled by what Foucault (1980: 131, 133) calls a '"political economy" of truth' or a '"régime" of truth'. Here, '"truth" is to be understood as a system of ordered procedures for the production, regulation, distribution, circulation and operation of statements' (Foucault 1980: 133). In turn, this is 'linked in a circular relation with systems of power which produce and sustain it, and to effects of power which it induces and which extend it' (ibid.). This is an autogenerative system that feeds on and reproduces understandings about the 'truth' of advertising – defined primarily as its assumed manipulative reach – whilst at the same time shielding the advertising industry from alternative truth claims about advertising and its social impact. Such interventions by regulatory bodies into the circuits of belief in and about advertising have material effects: they give added discursive weight to beliefs such as the powerfully persuasive effect of advertising's textual address, thus regenerating such beliefs despite very little 'proof' of those effects. Another ironic effect of the regulatory drive is that media coverage given to controversial campaigns can benefit agencies and their clients by drawing more attention to the advertisements and product. Yet the 'noise' or media attention created by contro-versial campaigns also provides the media with a platform to criticize advertising and to call for further regulation. I explore these issues more fully in the next chapter on advertising agencies, while in the following section, I examine the role of trade associations and other organizations in the discursive construction of advertising.

Instituting beliefs: trade associations and non-governmental organizations

Trade associations and other organizations that either support or critique advertising, draw on and reproduce beliefs in and about advertising for a range of commercial and political reasons. One coalition of groups that has a mandate to intervene in these circuits of belief and promote the interests of the advertising industry comprises the industry's own trade associations. The Advertising Association is a federation representing the interests of the advertising industry in the UK and its position on advertising issues directs those of two other key trade associations – the Institute for Practitioners in Advertising and the Incorporated Society of British Advertisers. The remit of the AA (2002: 1) is, 'to promote and protect the rights, responsibilities and role of advertising in the UK'. A key strategy of the AA, ISBA and IPA over many years has been to support 'responsible self-regulation' and to dissuade the British government and the European Union from instituting statutory regulation. With this remit, the trade organizations discursively construct the status and role of advertising in certain key ways: they present the effectiveness of advertising self-regulation; they argue that advertising's effects are less clear-cut and less insidious than commonly perceived; and they argue that advertising as free (commercial) speech should be protected from regulation.

As I have outlined, advertising self-regulation has long been a central issue for the industry and also for pressure groups which advocate more central control. As Geoff Russell, spokesperson of Institute for Practitioners in Advertising, told me in an interview, 'the advertising industry as a whole has tended to favour self-regulation as being a means whereby you can get effective control over what is actually advertised quickly, a way which corresponds to market change'. Similarly, the Incorporated Society of British Advertisers (2001: 1) follows the lead of the Advertising Association to work to 'promote the importance of advertising in driving competition in our economy, to promote the argument for self-regulation of commercial communications, especially in the light of the changing media environment, and – always – to defend the freedom of businesses to advertise responsibly'. This promotion of the industry as responsible, and self-regulation as cost-effective and flexible, has been the driving force behind many of the associations' initiatives. For instance, following a 1991 challenge by the European Commission, the Advertising Association played a key role in setting up the European Advertising Standards Alliance in order to demonstrate the effectiveness of self-regulation. The issue becomes more pointed with regard to commodities such as alcohol and tobacco. A position paper on advertising alcohol submitted by the Advertising Association to the Department of Health on 4 March 1999 argues that self-regulation is,

- cost-effective, fast, flexible, and can keep pace with developments;
- honoured in the spirit and the letter, engenders consensus, reverses the burden of proof;
- independent, harnesses industry and consumer expertise, preserves independence and is preventative;
- exclusively funded by the industry.

(Advertising Association 1999b: 5–6)

The trade associations also cite studies of advertising to support their position. For example, a study by Calfee (1997) that is very sympathetic to free market principles is cited by some of the associations in their submissions to government or in their press releases. Calfee (1997: 91) argues that the self-regulatory system in the UK is 'the most elaborate and arguably the most effective self-regulation system in the world'. Indeed, advertising benefits consumers more than producers as it triggers self-correcting market forces, whilst regulation favours producers over consumers. In this way, formal or statutory regulation over-extends its reach and 'victimizes consumers' (Calfee 1997: 89).

In another strand of the associations' discourse, the power of advertising to impact upon sales of commodities and upon society more generally is challenged. Contrary to the popular conception of advertising as a highly powerful tool that can, if practised skilfully, generate large increases in sales, the associations highlight the ambiguity of advertising's effects. The most prominent form this claim takes is that in mature markets, where various brands of a product have been long-established, advertising does not so much encourage new consumers to purchase the product as encourage existing consumers to change brands of that product. In this account, advertising does not increase the overall consumption of a product, but rather increases the share of the market for a particular brand or merely reinforces consumers' loyalty to their chosen brand. Whilst this analysis applies to all products in mature markets, controversial commodities such as alcohol and tobacco are defended most vigorously by this argument. In the Select Committee on Health's (2000: 1) minutes of evidence, a memorandum from British American Tobacco cites this as the preferred defence: 'British American Tobacco believes that cigarette advertising does not cause people to take up smoking. Simply put, cigarette advertising has two purposes – to maintain brand loyalty and to encourage smokers to switch brands.' In a response to government consultation documents of the draft Tobacco Regulations of 1999, the Advertising Association (1999a: 2) argued that, 'advertising in this market is a strategic tool, largely used by premium brands, in their competition for market share in a declining market'. And in a paper submitted to the Department of Health on alcohol advertising, the AA argued that 'there is little or no overall impact on total category consumption as a result of brand advertising'.

In a different approach, the third key defence of advertising is that of free speech. To support its stated aims of promoting and protecting 'the rights, responsibilities and role of advertising in the UK', Advertising Association (2002: 1) draws on Article 10 of the European Convention on Human Rights that 'recognises commercial freedom of speech as a right, alongside political and artistic freedoms of speech'. In the USA, general issues of free speech are protected by the First Amendment, although the defence of advertising as commercial free speech is not straightforward. For example, the 1971 US ban on broadcast advertising for cigarettes could not be challenged by the tobacco companies' right to free speech in the First Amendment as the airwaves are held to be public property and therefore subject to regulation for the general good (Kluger 1996). Free speech does not have the same status in British law. However, the European Convention on Human Rights now offers the advertising industry and client companies an opportunity to defend advertising as free commercial speech, an approach which is now often deployed in support of controversial advertising. In a book called *Ads and Fags: The Many Cases Against Banning Advertising*, the Advertising Association again refers to the Convention, asserting that 'free speech is free speech, whether it is religious, political, artistic or commercial' (1994: 5). In the same memorandum cited above, British American Tobacco argues that 'freedom of commercial speech is a basic principle of open markets'. It remains to be seen how successful this strategic defence of advertising will be in battles still being fought over rights to advertise in the EU, but it is clear that the issue of individual and commercial freedoms holds a high discursive charge. In a study published by the Institute for Economic Affairs in the UK, Hugh High argues that restrictions on tobacco and tobacco advertising represent an attempt to,

> restrict individual freedom to choose and restrict freedom of information. Only those with a disdain for the rights of individuals and who wish to substitute decision-making by the 'Nanny, or Orwellian, State' for decisions by free and independent individuals would support such restrictions.
>
> (High 1999: 117)

This is an interesting inversion in which attempts to curb advertising, rather than advertising and its imagined power to manipulate free will, are seen to represent an

Orwellian form of control in the interests of the state. Indeed, debates for and against tobacco and alcohol advertising very much hinge on these articulations of a dichotomy between freedom and control. The Tobacco Manufacturers Association (2001: 1), which is a trade association for UK companies (and American associate members), argues that it does not 'promote smoking in general, but it defends the freedom of adults to smoke if they so choose'. Groups that campaign for restrictions on tobacco and alcohol often do so on the basis of advertising's imagined curtailment of individuals' freedom. The Institute of Alcohol Studies (2001: 1) in the UK specifically targets advertising as a linchpin of its drive to control alcohol use. It makes a direct, although unsupported, claim that advertising images induce young people to drink at an early age, and claims that the advertising industry's marketing practices are now 'out of control' and their voluntary codes are 'not working': 'corporate greed lies at the heart of the drink industry's cynical manipulation of their voluntary codes of advertising practice'. Groups such as the World Health Organization (WHO) do not frame the issue of tobacco and tobacco advertising as a matter of freedom, but as a matter of necessary control. WHO (2000: 1) has for several years placed tobacco control at the forefront of its concerns and has produced a Framework Convention on Tobacco Control as 'a new legal instrument that could address issues as diverse as tobacco advertising and promotion, agricultural diversification, smuggling, taxes and subsidies'. As previously noted, this Convention was agreed by all 192 members of WHO in May 2003. WHO recognizes that tobacco control distils a wide range of issues and concerns that cannot be reduced solely to a ban on tobacco advertising. Whilst a study in which the World Bank worked in association with WHO recommends a comprehensive, world-wide ban on tobacco advertising, it is also noted that a number of other issues such as smuggling and higher taxation are key (World Bank 1999). However, it is advertising that forms the central target of these multiple concerns in the public discourse of WHO (2001: 1): a press release quotes the Director General as saying, 'tobacco addiction is a communicated disease – communicated through advertising, promotion and sponsorship'. The critiques and defences of advertising – particularly the defence that advertising merely encourages brand switching rather than initiating new consumers – are far from new (see Leiss *et al.* 1990). What is new in Britain, the EU and the practices of WHO are the legislative developments around advertising for 'dangerous commodities' such as tobacco. These shifts represent an important site of analysis for the construction of advertising as a cultural and economic form.

Legislating advertising

Legislation forms another nexus through which beliefs in and about advertising are circulated, reformed and recirculated. But this is not an entirely new phenomenon for, as I outlined at the beginning of this chapter, legislating advertising has had a long history and the nineteenth century in particular saw a proliferation of restrictions. In the more recent past, certain key statutory regulations about tobacco advertising were put in place: restrictions on tobacco advertising were first imposed in 1964 in the UK when manufacturers stopped advertising on television before 9 p.m.; a total ban on television advertising for cigarettes came into place in 1965; radio advertising for tobacco was banned in the early 1970s. Aligned with this legislative drive, the contemporary political climate also highlights tobacco advertising as point of intervention into what are seen as controversial and dangerous forms of consumption. The UK Labour government had a manifesto commitment in the 1997 general election to ban tobacco advertising and in the 1998 White Paper *Smoking Kills*, the government reaffirmed its commitment to a ban (UK Government 1998). The Tobacco Advertising and Promotion Bill was introduced to the House of Commons in December 2000 and to the House of Lords in July 2001 (UK Government 2001). It proposed a ban of all tobacco advertising and sponsorship except internal tobacco trade communications and included provisions to ban brand diversification (or 'brand-stretching') in which a company might indirectly market its brand of cigarettes by promoting a clothing or accessory range of the same name. The Bill passed its second reading in late 2002 and came into force on 14 February 2003.

These concerns about advertising in general, and tobacco advertising in particular, are also being played out at a European level. The Tobacco Advertising Directive 98/43/EC was adopted by the EU in July 1998 and required Member States to phase out all tobacco advertising, including promotion and sponsorship, by 1 October 2006. However, the Directive was challenged and taken to the European Court of Justice by tobacco companies, other trading companies, and by the German Government with the result that it was declared unlawful in October 2000. In December 2002, the Tobacco and Advertising Directive 2001/0119 (COD), which aims to ban tobacco advertising in the press and tobacco sponsorship, was agreed. My concern in this section is less with the detail of these on-going legislative procedures or their outcomes, and more with the discourses they draw on and generate about the nature, role and effects of advertising. In parallel to the organizations discussed in the previous section, it is recognized in many UK government and European Union documents on tobacco control that advertising is only one element of the promotional mix. A European Commission (2001: 1) draft proposal for a Directive on the Advertising of Tobacco Products and Related Sponsorship states that, 'although it is not universally accepted that advertising has been shown to be uniquely and directly responsible for people trying out smoking or getting addicted to the habit, the fact remains that it does play a fundamental role in promoting tobacco products'. The Commission cites no studies or theoretical frameworks to support the claim that advertising plays a fundamental role in promotion, nor does it elaborate the precise nature of this role. In a similar way, the UK government's (1998) White Paper *Smoking Kills* argues that an end to tobacco advertising is seen as a 'cornerstone' to any project aimed at reducing smoking without detailing any precise arguments about the role and effects of advertising. The default position in these debates is the self-evidence of advertising's power. Yet despite the broad scope of these claims, the draft Tobacco Advertising and Sponsorship Bill states that banning tobacco advertising and sponsorship will effect an estimated long-term reduction in tobacco consumption of just 2.5 per cent

(Department of Health 2002: 12). These documents draw their rhetoric force from well-established popular beliefs that advertising is powerful. In this context, the self-regulation of advertising and the conduct of advertising agencies receive a great deal of critical attention. In the response to the Health Select Committee's (2000: 2) Second Report on the Tobacco Industry and the Health Risks of Smoking, the UK government cites sections from the Select Committee's recommendations which argue that voluntary agreements have not worked and have merely served the advertising industry's interests: 'regulations have been seen as hurdles to be overcome or side-stepped; legislation banning advertising as a challenge, a policy to be systematically undermined by whatever means possible'. Furthermore, 'advertising agencies have connived in promoting tobacco consumption' and 'have used their creative talents to undermine Government policy and evade regulation'. This is a more strongly worded version of many academic studies' arguments that the 'scope [of self-regulation] is limited, its reach is incomplete, and its methods are only partially effective' (Boddewyn 1992: 16).

Addressing this critique, the British government required a number of advertising agencies that worked on tobacco accounts to submit documentation about their campaigns to the Health Select Committee in July 1999. These documents included internal memorandums, client briefs (an outline of advertiser's aims for a campaign), creative briefs (agencies' initial outlines of the aims and tone of the campaign to help direct creatives), advertising budgets, and market research reports.[3] Hastings and MacFadyen (2000a; 2000b) were part of a centre funded by the Cancer Research Campaign that advised the Select Committee as to which documents to demand, and also produced a series of questions to direct the analysis of the documents: Does tobacco advertising affect consumption as well as brand share? Does advertising target young people? What part does sponsorship play? What other forms of promotion are there, and what part do they play? In their analysis, the authors considered many documents that detailed the everyday business of the agency, such as minutes of meetings, uninteresting or irrelevant. In contrast, they considered that 'the creative briefs and qualitative market research were extremely revealing, not so much in what they said but in what they assumed about the four questions' (Hastings and MacFadyen 2000a: 366). Yet I suggest that the analyses presented by Hastings and MacFadyen reveal not so much the 'hidden truths' of advertising, but rather the many academic assumptions about advertising's role and effects.

In analysing the documentation from advertising agencies, Hastings and MacFadyen consistently take at face value the claims made by agencies about their power to target specific groups, the accuracy of market research, and the agencies' ability to create campaigns that will increase sales. These claims, as I detail in the next chapter, should be seen in context of promotional rhetoric produced by agencies in order to maintain and generate business in a highly competitive market. To illustrate – Hastings and MacFadyen argue that the documents reveal a clear desire on the part of client companies to increase overall tobacco consumption as well as brand share. They cite examples of proposed tactics, such as creating campaigns that target (existing) consumers by supporting the beleaguered smoker and their right to choose. One agency document that they isolate pitches the idea that 'as smokers become more and more persecuted, they look to advertising as a friend' (cited in Hastings and MacFadyen 2000a: 367). There is certainly evidence that anti-smoking sentiment in USA in 1980s led Philip Morris to champion smoker's rights and challenge what they called discrimination against smokers (Jackall and Hirota 2000). But whilst it may be clear that the tobacco industry, and indeed many other industries, may *wish* to increase overall consumption of their product not just their brand's share of the market, it is not clear that any specific tactics proposed by advertising agencies will achieve this result. The proposed strategy of advertising 'befriending' the persecuted smoker may have sinister undertones that chime well with the general perception of advertising's manipulative role. But the agency's *claim* of its efficiency does not unambiguously translate into successful targeting of those consumers. As I go on to outline, the effects of advertising are widely recognized by agencies and their clients to be highly ambiguous and difficult to isolate. Hastings and MacFadyen (2000a: 369) also highlight the issue of subliminal advertising and cite an agency's pitch for Silk Cut cigarettes' sponsorship of sports events: 'at each event the level of Silk Cut branding is intended to be subliminal, with no direct reference to Silk Cut cigarettes'. Hastings and MacFadyen do not recognize the status of this rhetoric as a promotional pitch from the creative team of the agency to persuade their colleagues of the merit of their approach or a promotional effort on behalf of an agency to persuade their clients of their creative and commercial skills. Such rhetoric does not translate unambiguously into successful persuasive practice. Rather, Hastings and MacFadyen see such practitioners' accounts as clear evidence of agencies' abilities to 'get round the defences of their "wary" and media literate young targets' (ibid.) by using the kind of depth manipulation that Vance Packard (1957) made (in)famous in both academic and advertising agency circles. As I have argued, the efficacy and even evidence of the use of subliminal advertising has long been debunked. In effect, subliminal advertising has become something of a mythical beast with mysterious powers, functioning as a trope for a range of concerns about advertising. Here, Hastings and MacFadyen fix onto the agency's use of the term 'subliminal' in their pitch and invest it with the weight of popular perceptions of advertising's sinister, manipulative powers. In contrast to the depth of this claim, I would argue that the agency's pitch refers on a more mundane and modest level to the subtle or cryptic forms of address that have long been common in tobacco advertising and that cannot be seen to translate directly into increased sales of the product.[4]

Hastings and MacFadyen's analysis is particularly significant as it is cited as evidence of advertising's invasive power in the consultation document of the Tobacco Advertising and Promotion Bill (Department of Health 2002). But their account is also typical of many approaches to advertising that draw on and perpetuate general perceptions of advertising that circulate in popular, political and academic arenas. In straightforwardly accepting the claims that advertising agencies make about their capacities to affect sales and influence minds, Hastings and MacFadyen risk fetishizing the power of advertising. In the next chapter,

I suggest that these claims by agencies are better understood as self-promotional rhetoric aimed at generating the belief amongst clients that a particular agency can successfully promote the cigarette brand despite severe restrictions as to format, site and content of tobacco advertising and sponsorship. Agencies attempt this rhetorical feat by drawing precisely on the widespread and unsubstantiated perception of the highly manipulative powers of advertising epitomized in so-called subliminal advertising. Hastings and MacFadyen do not recognize this self-perpetuating circuit of beliefs and claims, and whilst they acknowledge that advertising represents only one element of the mix of practices that promote a product – including marketing, pricing, distribution, package design, point of sales promotions – advertising consistently takes the brunt of their criticism. Hence they recommend comprehensive statutory regulation of advertising, 'with the overt aim of removing all tobacco marketing' (2000a: 370), and reserve a great deal of contempt for those working in the advertising industry: 'one is left with the inescapable conclusion, that given the greatest threat to public health this country has faced since the great plague, these people are having fun, making money and showing absolutely no concern for the consequences of their actions' (Hastings and MacFadyen 2000b: 5). Hastings and MacFadyen's motivations are clearly well-directed concerns about public health, but their blunt analytic approach to agencies' promotional rhetoric risks overlooking the more complex and contingent ways in which advertising as an institution impacts upon consumption patterns, social values and the restructuring of social taxonomies. Analyses such as theirs fail to achieve an understanding of how discourses generated by institutions such as government, the EU, the advertising industry (and academics) contribute to the discursive construction of advertising as a commercial practice and representational form.

In this chapter, I have explored discourses of advertising circulating in and between regulatory bodies such as the Advertising Standards Authority, the advertising trade associations of the Institute for Practitioners in Advertising and the Advertising Association, and NGOs such as the World Health Organization, UK legislation on advertising, and European Union legislation. It is certainly possible to track similarities or resonances in the logics of these discourses despite their different aims and agendas. Debates about advertising effects are played out in relation to market share and both regulatory stances and more laissez-faire approaches draw on freedom as their pivotal principle: freedom from the manipulation of advertising; freedom to promote goods; freedom to consume as we wish; freedom from harmful commodities. Promotional discourses operate across all levels: the ASA promotes self-regulation by aiming to demonstrate the effectiveness of its monitoring; the UK government is eager to be seen to be promoting health by banning tobacco advertising; clients are promoting their products and brands. All groups make arguments based on general perceptions of advertising rather than rigorously researched analysis. But one key resonance that I want to highlight here is the way in which advertising regulation, legislation, trade associations and other NGOs figure advertising as a site of animation. Advertising is imagined to activate commodities, facilitating dangerous connections between consumers and those commodities. This concern is most explicit in relation to commodities such as tobacco and alcohol and the addictive consumption practices they are thought to elicit. But the principle that drives this concern is a more general understanding of advertising as a dangerously disruptive force or social pathogen. In Chapter 1, I explored how controversies about the burgeoning consumer society of the nineteenth century took as one focus the disruption of social type and specification that consuming practices such as oniomania represented. More worrisome still, such deviant consuming practices actively shifted the very modes of categorizing the social realm and demarcating the distinctions between person and thing, consumer and commodity. This perception of its power to *animate*, I suggest, forms one key element of contemporary concerns about advertising. In attributing a form of agency or animating capacity to advertising texts, contemporary regulatory and industry discourses cast advertising as a prime actor in a new bio-politics. Supplementary to Foucault's understanding, this bio-politics focuses the regulatory regime not only on the control of the species-being through fertility, health and birth rates, but also focuses controlling efforts on the strict demarcations between persons and things. The perceived dynamic relations between persons and things form a general social concern, but take a specific institutional force in the regulatory imperatives and commercial practices of advertising. Ironically, in animating advertising – or attributing advertising an animating force – the regulatory dis-courses further trouble these segregated understandings of agentic human subjects and non-agentic objects and commodities.

In this dynamic, advertising regulations (and discourses generated to promote self-regulation rather than statutory regulation) give form to abstract notions of advertising. They fix the multi-stranded flow of all that constitutes advertising – including market research, promotional practices such as design, commercial imperatives, audience reception, intra-industry competition – and cast the adver-tising text itself as essence or defining core of advertising as a social, political and economic institution. In parallel, analyses such as those of Hastings and MacFadyen (2000a, 2000b) fix on practitioners' rhetoric and market research documents, claiming that they represent the truth of advertising and its effects. These approaches halt the dynamics of the flow of elements and offer an artificially static under-standing of what advertising is and what its effects might be. This limited, contrived presentation of advertising as pure text is endorsed by advertising agencies, trade associations, agencies' clients and the regulatory regimes of the state for a complex of reasons. It is in the interests of trade associations and advertising agencies to demonstrate the efficacy of self-regulation as a form of control, thus reducing or eliminating the need for more stringent statutory regulations. Siting the crux of advertising's force in the text offers a convenient way of delimiting advertising's potential purchase. It offers a manageable way of demonstrating responsible commercial practice by regulating those advertising texts whilst excluding other practices or areas of promotion from the regulatory gaze. State interests in regulating advertising also latch onto the text of the advertisement as a site of manageable and high-profile intervention. Driving through regulations on tobacco advertising, for instance, has presented a tactical opportunity for the UK government to demonstrate a commitment to improving the nation's health whilst also gaining acclaim for curbing what is seen as a corrosive force on society. Indeed, regulating advertising images is a simpler and far less costly option than attempting to alter people's consumption patterns directly or addressing complex socio-economic issues of taxation on 'dangerous commodities', smuggling, and cross-border co-operation on regulatory consumption practices. It is by drawing on popular perceptions of the wide manipulative reach of advertising that the government has been able to achieve this impact. In effect, the circuits of belief in and about advertising actively constitute advertising as a social, political and economic institution. Thus, beliefs about advertising 'substantialize' it and generate its social form. For instance, when complaints about advertisements are made to the Advertising Standards Authority they are grounded in understandings that advertisements 'do' things or in some ways act upon the individual or upon society, for example, in artificially manipulating consuming practices, eroding social values, or perpetuating social stereotypes. Directed by its remit to promote an image of industry responsibility and deflect further statutory regulation, the ASA takes any such complaint very seriously and details advertisements' textual infringements of its Codes. In addition, the ASA uses as benchmarks the many surveys it carries out about public standards of taste and decency and public understandings of advertising. The ASA thus explicitly incorporates generally-circulating beliefs about advertising into its own regulatory processes and adjudications. In addition, by assessing the impact of any advertising campaign using the limited and ambiguous scope of textual infringements instituted by its arbitrary Codes, the ASA actively perpetuates beliefs of advertising as a highly powerful social force. This is instanced in the general perception that 'advertising must be powerful, or it would not be regulated'.

Moreover, in focusing almost exclusively on advertising texts, regulations have unforeseen impacts. As I argued in the previous chapter, the specific distinctions instituted between person and thing in the nineteenth century distributed agency and animation between those categories according to a principle of scarcity. Thus, agency was accorded to the classification of 'person' in direct proportion to its denial of the classification of 'thing': this was a zero-sum game in which any concession of agency to things translated into a worrying erosion of the agency of persons. The contemporary regulatory focus on advertising texts also laments the potential loss of human agency and the commensurate gain of the material world. But it also has rather different effects, for contrary to the distribution of agency, no principle of scarcity is thought to operate in the distribution of meaning: understandings of advertising's effects on the circulation of meaning do not function in terms of a zero-sum game. Advertising is imagined to destroy or erode meaning (see Goldman 1992) or, in contrast, is thought to encourage a proliferation of meanings that saturate the social field. In this second account, the massive multiplication of meaning is thought to foster a need for specialists with expert knowledges who offer guidance in making choices in this overwhelming arena of meanings (see Featherstone 1991). Alternatively, this proliferation of meanings is interpreted as rendering meaning empty or evacuating it of it sense (see Baudrillard 1988). My concern here is to highlight how, by focusing on the textual element of the advertising institution, regulations cast meaning (in contrast to agency) as an infinitely elastic category that is variously subject to erosion, compression or expansion. This broad understanding of advertising's potential effects is mirrored in agencies' and clients' fears that bans on certain advertising, such as for tobacco, will have a contagious effect on other products. That is, there are concerns that stricter regulation of advertising in some areas will expand its scope and proliferate its regulatory regime.[5] Thus, the (unsuccessful) battle to prevent statutory regulation of tobacco advertising in the UK was not fought solely by tobacco companies and agencies that had tobacco accounts; broader concerns about the freedom to advertise were implicated in the terms of the attack.

In parallel, the new statutory regulation of tobacco advertising in the UK – that aims to curb the promotion of that product – is currently engendering a *proliferation* of promotional practices for tobacco products. Brand-sharing, 'brand-stretching' or trademark diversification, whereby companies advertise tobacco brands through other products such as clothing, is banned by the Tobacco Advertising and Promotion Bill. But other novel avenues for promotion are being explored: there are discussions about the possibility of 'stealth marketing' practices by tobacco companies such as funding websites that obliquely promote tobacco use.[6] For instance, it is reported that British American Tobacco invested £2.5m into citygobo.com, a website guide to clubs, bars and restaurants. A BAT-owned brand, Rothmans, has already launched a 'pub quiz' form of promotion in the UK in which smokers are encouraged to contact the company with answers to a series of questions found in cigarette packs. This tactic cleverly exploits a loophole in the new legislation by which a company may contact consumers with promotional material if the consumer has first contacted them and asked for information. Other strategies are being explored by companies: 'viral marketing', in which mini-ads are sent via email, and the creation of 'brand experiences' in areas of airports (which are not subject to such rigid regulation), are only two instances of what will certainly be an expanding list of commercial tactics. This epitomizes the ironies of promotion, novelty and regulation: an outright ban on tobacco advertising and most direct marketing paradoxically encourages the development of sophisticated new ways of interesting consumers in 'dangerous commodities'.

In addition, by distilling concerns about advertising down to the text of advertisements, legislative moves and self-regulatory bodies paradoxically expand the field of 'addictive' or dangerous consumption. Instead of controlling, containing and strictly circumscribing the terms of what counts as unhealthy or addictive consumption practices in relation to the advertising of tobacco and alcohol, the regulations actually open up the terms of such practices making them available in new ways to redefinition. In Foucaultian terms, imperatives to control and regulate can be seen as actively *producing* consumption forms and subject positions rather than merely *repressing* a particular (dangerous) consumption practice. But I would argue that such control does not only encourage a proliferation of precisely that which it seeks to curtail; it also disaggregates those substances or practices that are understood as addictive or pathological and makes them more mobile. In shifting the imagined site of pathology and addiction from the substance itself to its advertising – to the level of representation – the regulatory bodies in fact enable those discourses to circulate in new ways. By pinpointing advertising's social impact in the texts themselves, the regulations focus and intensify understandings of advertising as a dangerous representational form that erodes the distinct classifications of 'person' and 'thing' and fosters unhealthy or 'addictive' relations between consumers and commodities. By casting tobacco advertising as threatening and drawing attention to its disruption of type and taxonomy, regulations thus escalate a sense that *all* advertising threatens the classificatory orders of the social realm. This expanded scope of concerns empowers advertising and marketing to further proliferate promotional practices and hence amplify the allied effect of taxonomic breakdown. So although the regulatory bodies focus their attention on advertising imagery and text, they in fact succeed in *broadening* the scope of compulsion and of consumption. They enable new connections between materialities, images and practices to be made and potential new modes of consumption to be formed. In Chapter 5, I explore how these connections allow a more fluid movement of perceptions of compulsion between sites, practices, institutional structures and identities that may enable us to inhabit new subject positions precisely based around 'bad consumption'. Indeed, we frequently hear that we are now addicted to video games, addicted to reading, addicted to relationships, addicted to welfare provision, addicted to sex and so on. I will argue that advertising's regulatory practices and how they connect to the beliefs and commercial practices of advertising agencies are important in facilitating these expanding circuits. And, in turn, these new circuits are key in defining what it means to consume, and particularly what it means to consume pathologically, addictively or healthily. The following chapter aims to address some of these issues by attending more subtly to the complex of beliefs, promotional rhetoric, and practices that occur in advertising agencies.

3 Advertising agencies
Commercial reproduction and the management of belief

In their famous analysis of culture, Adorno and Horkheimer (1997: 162) accorded advertising a prime role in the reproduction of capitalism claiming that advertising has 'permeated the idiom – the "style" – of the culture industry', and now functions as its 'elixir of life'. It has become such an all-embracing presence that 'advertising and the culture industry merge technically as well as economically' (Adorno and Horkheimer 1997: 163). Whilst many aspects of their account of culture have been rejected as schematic and deterministic, their approach to advertising has maintained its resonance in the popular and academic imagination. Indeed, their understanding of advertising as a key driving force of the capitalist culture industry has set the tone for many contemporary analyses of promotional practices. Articulating this critical approach, Deleuze has claimed that 'marketing is now the instrument of social control and produces the arrogant breed who are our masters' (1995: 181). As I have argued in previous chapters, debates about advertising channel a wide range of social and political concerns and elicit some interesting rhetorical flourishes (particularly in academic critiques). Many of these critiques have been directed at advertising texts and the circulation of promotional signs; for instance, Goldman (1992: 34) argues that 'the advertising industry can be viewed as a system for the production and exchange of commodity-signs'. In this chapter, I suggest that the reality of the advertising industry both falls short of and exceeds Goldman's claim in important ways. In my own analysis of advertising practitioner's accounts of their professional role and their beliefs about advertising, I argue that the advertising industry functions neither so systematically nor so efficiently: it is not an infallible commercial machine, inexorably generating and disseminating consistently persuasive promotional tools. Instead, the industry operates on a more contingent basis, not so much driving cultural change as responding or reacting to it; not so much actively generating a culture of consumption as defensively promoting agencies' own skills in a crowded, competitive marketplace. In parallel, the industry does not merely produce and exchange advertisements as 'commodity-signs'; agencies attempt to institute a system of commercial exchange based on their knowledge and skills in competition with other commercial knowledge providers such as management and branding consultants. In this chapter, I explore how the advertising industry is less the monolithic capitalist apparatus as suggested by some accounts, and more a complex and provisional circulation of commercial rhetoric with short-term, ambiguous impact. Indeed, in contrast to purely text-based analyses of advertisements, ethnographic or interview-based accounts of advertising such as my own have tended to be wary of claims about the over-arching economic power or social effects of advertising (see Leiss *et al*. 1990; Miller 1997; Moeran 1996; Slater 1989; Tunstall 1964).

The research for this chapter focuses on interview-based material from major London advertising agencies. There are clearly limitations to such an approach which, unlike an ethnography, cannot track the development of campaigns and detail decision-making processes and client–agency relations. In addition, my study does not include an analysis of media buyers in agencies who segment the target market according to media form and buy media space for advertisements. To supplement my analysis, I draw on several ethnographic studies (Miller 1997; Moeran 1996; Tunstall 1964). However, the following analysis is necessarily limited in scope and provides only a partial account of the everyday commercial activities of agencies. But my concern here is not centred on providing an exhaustive mapping of the practices of agencies. Drawing on my own and others' analyses, I aim to explore the circulation of beliefs in and about advertising and the promotional imperatives that frame these multiple and at times contradictory discourses. This is an important element of commercial practice as practitioners' own perceptions and their own beliefs in and about advertising feed back into their practices and the campaigns they produce. I am not, then, attempting to isolate proofs about advertising's effects or to make claims about the essential truths of advertising. Rather, my aim is to examine the '"political economy" of truth' that constitutes advertising (Foucault 1980: 131). This economy of beliefs and truth claims about advertising circulates through many points of tension: the politics and identity of each agency; the promotional claims made by agencies competing for heightened profile and client accounts; the power struggles between Account Managers, Planners and Creatives within agencies; and the management of power relations between agencies and their clients. I have assessed the interview material from two key analytic angles. First, I have considered the practitioners' accounts as broadly representative of advertising practice. I feel confident in attributing this status to their accounts as they generally tallied with other ethnographic studies that have both tracked advertising practice and analysed rhetoric about advertising. Second, I have analysed the material to explore the promotional imperatives for agencies and for individual practitioners and how the circulation of these (self-) promotional accounts actively constitute advertising as a social and economic form. The productive tension present in these two methodological approaches mirrors the tension present within the agencies' own discourses and practices and is indeed constitutive of the commercial form that is advertising.

To examine the ways in which practitioners discursively construct advertising as a set of practice, images, knowledges and ideas, I interviewed Account Managers, Account Planners and Creatives at several major London agencies. All the interviews took place in January 2002 at the agencies' London offices and each lasted between forty-five minutes and two hours. In line with my argument about agencies' and practitioners' self-promotional imperative, every practitioner except one expressly asked to be named and their agency identified. The individual profile of practitioners and of agencies is clearly key in the promotional matrix that is the advertising industry – evidently, practitioners subscribe to the maxim that all publicity is good publicity. The practitioners I interviewed were Matthew Anderson, Senior Creative and member of the Board at Partners BDDH; Paul Gardener, Account Director at Rainey Kelly Campbell Roalfe/Y&R; John Gregg, Global Planner at Ogilvy and Mather; Vicki Maguire, Senior Creative and Creative Director on three accounts at Ogilvy and Mather; Steve Nicholls, Senior Creative and member of the Board at Partners BDDH; Peter St Amour, Account Manager at Ogilvy and Mather; Mark Sell, Account Manager at Grey Worldwide; Nick Southgate, Account Planner at Ogilvy and Mather; an Account Manager at a major agency who wishes to remain anonymous. Creatives are art directors and copywriters who are responsible for generating ideas for the campaign and for producing the images and the copy (the spoken or written words in an advertisement). Account Planners write briefs for the Creatives that outline the scope and aims of the campaign, they analyse and prepare long-term strategy and liase with research companies. Account Managers are responsible for project management and finance and day-to-day contact with the client. Senior practitioners tend to be called Account Director, Creative Director etc. I also interviewed Claire Forbes, Head of Communications at the Advertising Standards Authority, Geoff Russell, spokesperson for the Institute of Practitioners in Advertising, and Tim Ambler of the London Business School. Ambler has worked in advertising and marketing since the 1970s, was involved in setting up the ASA, and has been a member of the Advertising Association's Council.

Advertising effects and agencies' self-promotional practices

In commercial, academic and popular accounts, the issue of effects on sales circulates as a key element in advertising's political economy of truth. The perceived effects function as a nexus around which advertising is criticized, regulated and defended. At the same time, claims about advertising's effects circulate as a currency with which individual advertising practitioners and agencies competitively promote their skills. As I have noted, one popular conception figures the advertising industry as a streamlined, commercial machine that effortlessly and inexorably produces powerfully effective advertisements. Resonating with a sense that advertising is intensely manipulative, such perceptions have great appeal and discursive impact but they are not based on any appreciation of the actual processes of advertising production or the complex, fragile commercial relations between agencies and their clients. For instance, the process of researching, planning, producing and editing a television commercial is fraught with difficulties, and there are no assurances that the completed advertisement will be either an artistic or a commercial success (Arlen 1980). Moreover, the relations between practitioners within an agency, and between agency and client, are far removed from the popular image of a lean, efficient machine that harmoniously integrates its diverse elements to effortlessly generate successful, persuasive advertising. In reality, there is rarely consensus in an agency about the proposed approach of a campaign and there is a constant process of negotiation and compromise between agency, client and media organization (Moeran 1996). The 'truth' of advertising practice and advertising effects is thus a provisional, complex affair. This is nowhere more evident than in the self-laudatory books written by the 'great men' of advertising (e.g. Bullmore 1991; Ogilvy 1964, 1983). Replete with anecdotes and words of commercial wisdom, the authors of these books lay claim to special knowledge about advertising and aggrandize the business of advertising to the status of profession. As another of these heroes of advertising says, such books 'all over-flow with gnomic maxims, which they claim, invariably result in effective advertising' (Fletcher 1999: 121). This is only partially true, for many such books openly acknowledge that advertising's effects are not guaranteed, nor are those effects easily identified. Discussing the benefits of research and the pre-testing of advertisements, David Ogilvy casts doubt on the popular perception of advertising's overwhelmingly successful powers and indicates that agencies and clients are only too aware of advertising's ambiguous effects:

> I sometimes wonder if there is a tacit conspiracy amongst clients, media and agencies to avoid putting advertising to such acid tests. Everyone involved has a vested interest in prolonging the myth that *all* advertising increases sales to some degree. It doesn't.
>
> (Ogilvy 1983: 9)

Of course, Ogilvy goes on to argue that his approach does indeed offer the secrets to successful advertising. But this self-promotional rhetoric does not detract from the overall significance of his account: agencies and their clients perceive advertising's effects to be ambiguous and often indeterminate.

This indeterminacy of effect has been recognized for many years in some of the more thoughtful and nuanced academic studies of advertising. Writing in 1964, Jeremy Tunstall argues that little is known about the effects of advertising and that in the context of other promotional forms such as packaging and pricing, advertising may only play a minor role in selling goods: 'the other variables are so many that in practice the single factor of advertising cannot usually be isolated and its effects precisely measured' (Tunstall 1964: 16). This early insight is echoed in later academic accounts, most notably of Michael Schudson (1993), who argues that both clients and agencies are painfully aware of advertising's ambiguous status and effects. In parallel journalistic accounts, both Clark (1990) and Stabiner (1993) relate numerous practitioner accounts that consistently acknowledge the imprecision in gauging the effects of their advertising. As I detail in later sections, my own interviews with advertising practitioners support, and indeed extend, these claims. Most practitioners in my study subscribe to the view that advertising does not have a direct and unambiguous effect on sales, as one Account Manager told me, 'a lot of people have tried to prove it but it's never been proven' (St Amour). I do not read such accounts by practitioners as defensive rhetoric to protect the advertising business from academic criticism. From my interviews, it became clear that practitioners are not in the least concerned about academics' opinions of them, instead investing their energy and efforts in the highly competitive career pathways of the business. On the contrary – as I argue in the next section – the structure of the advertising business is such that practitioners are more directed towards *talking advertising up*, or aggrandizing its putative capacities to increase sales and raise a company's profile. This imperative derives precisely from a recognition by agencies, and an abiding suspicion on the part of clients, that advertising is not the efficient commercial weapon characterized by common knowledge. Tim Ambler highlights the difficult position in which this knowledge places agencies: '[advertising] is just a tool which is used in different circumstances to do different things. . . . A very large amount of advertising doesn't increase sales even of its own brand. This is always an embarrassment for ad agencies – that the great majority of advertising doesn't have any effect on sales at all'. As Miller (1997) argues, this indeterminacy of effect provides agencies with their first challenge – to persuade clients to advertise at all. Many companies have noted with interest the success of their own products that have not been advertised and need to be persuaded that expensive advertising campaigns are the best use of limited resources.

Furthermore, advertising's primary aim may not be that of persuading consumers to buy the product. Schudson (1993) argues that advertising campaigns operate as promotional tools in multiple ways. For instance, when company executives make presentations to stockholders or potential investors, they always present the company's advertisements because, 'expensive, well-executed, and familiar ads convince the investors, as nothing in the black and white tables of assets and debits can, that the company is important and prosperous' (Schudson 1993: xiv). Increased numbers of, or increased input from, investors means augmented funds and a level of prosperity that could, paradoxically, be attributed to the influence of advertising. More funds may then be allocated to the advertising budget thus contributing to a self-fulfilling prophecy. In Schudson's compelling account, advertisements do not generate sales so much as sales generate advertisements. Agencies, then, are fully aware that it is not possible to isolate the effects of advertising from other promotional practices and they reflexively incorporate this knowledge into their commercial practices in significant ways.[1] Most popular and some academic analyses, however, do not recognize the commercial indeterminacy of advertising. In taking at face value the self-promotional claims generated by agencies, such understandings often attribute enormous power to advertising and malicious intent to advertising practitioners themselves. This problem has been recognized for some time, for as Pease (1958: 197) argues of American advertising in the period 1920–40, 'individual advertisers have scarcely been able to foresee or to anticipate the cumulative effects of what they do, and it would be difficult if not irrelevant to ascribe to them special motives or deliberate intentions for the ultimate social impact of advertising'.

One key mode through which practitioners incorporate the understanding of advertising's commercial indeterminacy into advertising practice is through the self-promotional discourses that individuals and agencies generate for competitive advantage. But the promotional imperative of agencies – and the promotional culture that it generates – is not new. In the nineteenth century, intense pressure to demonstrate their commercial worth directed agencies to promote an image of the industry's professionalism (Laird 1998; Marchand 1985; Ohmann 1996). Their promotional pamphlets emphasized 'efficiency, organization, specialization, planning' (Pope 1983: 176). But as Pope remarks of early twentieth-century agencies, the promotion of their commercial acumen and creative potential was an awkward blend:

> Agencies wanted national advertisers of branded products to see them as skilled, learned marketing counsellors. The sober, business-like visage was partially negated, however, by the fact that advertising was by no means the rational, closely-calculated investment advertising men claimed it was. The intuition, empathy, and verbal fluency agencies needed uneasily yoked to the rhetoric and values of business practice.
>
> (Pope 1983: 182)

The ambiguous status of advertising as a profession and as a kind of promotional 'science' remains a problem of legitimation for contemporary agencies. Agencies expend considerable effort in promoting themselves as a kind of management or promotional science with professionally trained employees, but the perception amongst practitioners themselves belies this. One Account Planner in my study told me:

> Certainly there's a fine line between a bespoke creative process and making it up as you go along, and it's a fine line that we have been known to walk the wrong side of. . . . Because there's so few places that training happens for certain jobs within the industry, there's a lot of guessing and making it up and coping.
>
> (Southgate, Account Planner)

This perception of advertising practitioners as rather poorly trained, if perhaps creative, individuals also filters through to potential clients of agencies. This means that agencies have to work even harder at self-promotion: they have a commercial imperative to promote an image of themselves as skilled commercial practitioners to clients which is just as strong as the imperative to promote an image of the client's products to consumers (see also Moeran 1996). Indeed, advertising is in a precarious commercial position: 'the advertising industry is characterized by work that is hard to specify and a product that is hard to evaluate' (Alvesson 1994: 542). Agencies are thus in a position of weakness relative to their clients due to the general awareness that there is no widely established means of measuring advertising's effectiveness (Kover and Goldberg 1995). No degree of skill or research can guarantee successful advertising and the large corporations that provide much of the industry's business hold the purse strings and the balance of power in the client–agency relationship. Additional uncertainties derive from the fact that clients can make decisions which agencies are unable to foresee, leaving agencies in a vulnerable and dependent position, whilst the creative process of generating ideas of advertisements is itself unpredictable (ibid.). All these factors combine to produce 'endemic insecurity' for agencies and a heavy dependence on clients (Pope 1983: 272).

In this context of insecurity, the issue of advertising's effects is used as a self-promotional resource in order to stabilize the uncertainties of the field and to attempt to redress the skewed power balance between clients and agencies. Thus, discourses about the effects of advertising are deployed as 'weapons of competition as well as legitimation and proof' (Slater 1989: 122). Here, the 'truth' of advertising effects is indeterminate and ultimately less significant than the discursive work to which claims about those effects are put. These instances of competitive self-promotion can take many forms; for instance, negotiating contracts of agreement between agencies and clients functions not only as an economic necessity but also as a cultural marker of distinction for the agency – the contracts operate as symbolic signifiers with which agencies defend and promote their status as skilled providers of commercial persuasion (Nixon 2002). In parallel, promotional rhetoric about advertising's effects and an agency's commercial skills is also deployed in order to gain legitimacy for the industry and business for the individual agency by drawing on clients' anxieties about successfully targeting the market and selling the product. In this rhetorical strategy, agencies attempt to allay producers' anxiety by framing themselves as intermediaries with special creative and promotional skills who can successfully identify and target consumers (Lury and Warde 1997). In this self-promotional practice, advertising is thus framed as a quasi-magical tool which only agencies can successfully deploy. So despite the knowledge circulating within the industry and amongst clients that advertising's effects are indeterminate – and that advertising can hardly be considered magically persuasive – advertising still retains its *image* as a powerful commercial tool. Agencies do indeed use advertising as a commercial tool, but it is one that promotes their agency and its skills first and foremost. In this scenario, both practitioners and clients actively contribute to the circuits of belief in and about advertising. They invest in a flexible relationship to truth claims about advertising and clients tend to share 'a general faith in advertising even when they couple it with specific doubts' (Schudson 1993: 127). This all contributes to one of the many paradoxes in advertising: if practitioners succeed in persuading clients (and of course regulators) that advertisements are effective, they expose advertising practice to intensified regulation and increased social criticism. Whereas if practitioners promote the message that advertisements have little impact (in response to regulators' claims of advertising's pernicious power), they are sending a message to potential clients that advertisements are likely to be commercially ineffective.

Despite analyses that demonstrate the ambiguous effects of advertising, there remains a belief in many academic studies that advertising 'works' in powerful and clear-cut ways (e.g. Goldman 1992). The commonsense view of advertising – represented in the way that pressure groups, regulatory bodies, legislation and some academics frame advertising – is that advertising practitioners use a range of underhand and highly effective techniques in order to manipulate the consumer. And indeed this discourse is one which circulates within agencies, albeit in rather more nuanced ways: 'we always talk about sneaking up on the consumer, catching them unawares . . . the idea is to get around that mental barrier of "I will not be manipulated"' (St Amour, Account Manager). But as I have argued, the objectives and claims in the rhetoric of the industry should not be taken at face value. Effectiveness cannot be read off from the discourses that advertising practitioners generate about their own skills, the skills of their agency, or about advertising in general. As the above quotation makes clear, *talking advertising up* is the key way in which advertising as a cultural and commercial form is constituted in the everyday practices of agencies. My interviews with practitioners reveal that talk is a key tactic deployed by agencies in order to manage the vulnerabilities of their practice. Talk, alongside other promotional forms and the investment in research techniques, is the currency that links the circuits of belief about advertising. It can be used to intervene in understandings of advertising and to substantiate agencies' status as skilled commercial intermediaries. When asked about the key characteristic required by an advertising practitioner, one Account Manager I interviewed replied, 'being articulate, because you spend a long time discussing things that there isn't a great deal to say about' (Anonymous). Advertising is certainly about persuasion, but as I have argued, much of the effort is expended in persuading the client to hire the agency and agree to the proposed campaign. For this reason, advertising has often been described as a 'people business' as it relies on the ability of individuals both to compose campaigns and to sell ideas to their clients. Ralph Hower (1949: 205) characterises the advertising agency as a commercial practice which, unlike a shop, 'has no goods on its shelves except experience, ideas, and ability'. This account of agencies in the early twentieth century remains current and is echoed in practitioners' own discourses: 'the only capital is thinking capital in an agency. There's nothing but people' (Gregg, Global Planner). The only capital that resides in agencies, then, is their ability to intervene in and direct circuits of belief about advertising that they achieve primarily through self-promotional discourses. These include websites, brochures, campaigns for the agency in the trade press, pitches to clients, but take as their linchpin promotional talk.

Regulation, promotional rhetoric and commercial practice

In the following section I explore these promotional discourses and analyse the material from my interviews for insights into the commercial practices of producing and pitching advertising campaigns. I argue that advertising is an industry based on discourse and discourse management in which practitioners create and recreate regimes of truth about advertising and their promotional skills within a competitive, commercial arena. The practitioners in my study do not merely circulate rhetoric about advertising – they operationalize their understandings of advertising, its role, its status, and its target markets in their practices and hence incorporate 'advertising talk' into advertising practice. My analysis focuses on regulation as it is a key point of tension in public, industry and clients' understandings of advertising: regulation attempts to manage advertising and its perceived effects, whilst practitioners attempt to manage the circuits of belief about advertising. The following sections explore the differing accounts presented by advertising practitioners about the status, role and effectiveness of advertising filtered through the issue of regulation.

Whilst the restriction or regulation of advertising is an issue that attracts a great deal of political and media attention, it became clear from my interviews that it is not in the foreground of most advertising agencies' everyday practices and discourses. As one Account Manager said, 'it's a background issue – it's not something we talk about over lunch' (Anonymous). For the practitioners, regulation is an issue that only comes into focus when there are problems with BACC clearance or a complaint has been made to the Advertising Standards Authority: 'it's just never discussed as an abstract thing . . . it only comes up when your ad can't go through' (Southgate, Account Planner). Unlike the BACC, the powers of the ASA are recognized to be very limited as they do not monitor advertisements before publication and only investigate a campaign once a complaint has been made. The ASA's main sanction against agencies and companies that consistently flout the regulations is a requirement that the ASA pre-vet all their advertisements before publication. This leads to a perception amongst practitioners that the ASA's influence is severely restricted: 'it was always called the toothless watchdog . . . the poster pre-vetting thing is probably the most power they have. Because with press ads, if they get pulled or banned, well, generally they've run their course anyway because it's a very long-winded procedure' (St Amour, Account Manager). By the time a successful complaints procedure for a press advertisement is complete, 'most advertising agencies can say "fine, you can have it" because by and large they're not going to return to that ad' (Gardener, Account Director). The ASA's deterrent is more effective for posters as these have a longer running time and therefore a campaign would be severely disrupted should the ASA require that an advertisement be removed. Yet practitioners do not generally view regulations as severe hindrances and it is this perception of the ASA's limited powers that guides the practices of agencies.

In my interviews, it was the Creatives who revealed themselves to be most concerned with the impact of regulations, especially the BACC Codes for broadcast advertisements that were considered to be overly restrictive. They were most irritated by what was perceived as the Codes' restriction on the creativity and innovation of their campaigns, an issue that came into sharp focus for the most controversial commodities such as alcohol and tobacco. A Creative expressed his frustration to me about what he called unnecessary restrictions. For him, these resulted in unrealistic depictions in advertisements that jarred with common knowledge about a particular product:

> Beer – we all know what it does. We're not allowed to tell you what it does to your body. . . . None of them [beer advertisements] is actually telling you anything about what you get in that can because you can't, you're not allowed to. . . . We wanted to do a Stella [beer] campaign which was, 'Stella. Brewed with real fighting hops', because you go and fight after you've had 4 pints of Stella!. . . . That didn't quite work [laughs].
>
> (Anderson, Senior Creative)

Practitioners are clearly frustrated by the limitations placed on them by the ASA, ITC and BACC Codes, and some deliberately set out to breach the Codes. This was a recognized trend amongst the practitioners I interviewed: 'a lot of campaigns that have been designed to generate the most controversy have been the ones that have been done on the lowest budgets, so the only way to actually get the noise is to create something which is actually going to create a stir . . . like Tango, FCUK' (St Amour, Account Manager). Both the Tango (a soft drink) and the FCUK (French Connection clothes company) campaigns created a great deal of controversy and media attention. This tactic can be doubly effective for in generating media attention, it targets and appeals to specific groups: 'the people who would be interested in those brands would be those who were interested in that kind of controversy' (St Amour, Account Manager). In this self-promotional industry, 'spin', 'media hype' and 'noise' are regarded as desirable, particularly by Creatives:

> This is one of the few industries probably where all publicity is good publicity. A lot of campaigns that get stick from the media are purely designed to get that kind of media attention. . . . If you've got a small campaign that you want to make a bit of noise about, you haven't got a lot of money, you do something either shocking or controversial so it's going to get talked about, it's going to get on Newsnight, it's going to get in the papers, your agency may get a slagging for bad taste or whatever . . . but, you know, you've upped that client's profile in a way that four or five times the media spend couldn't do. So a lot of it, to be perfectly honest, is calculated . . . The ad gets talked about, the ad appears in papers that you actually couldn't afford to buy the ad space in.
>
> (Maguire, Senior Creative)

Clearly, the fact that a campaign or an advertisement has been banned by the ITC, or a complaint about it upheld by the ASA, generates considerable media attention. Assuming that the client is not opposed to critical media attention, this represents good value for money – it is an advertisement for the advertisement. It is primarily Creatives who see the appeal of this, arguing that regulations stunt creativity and should be circumvented if at all possible. Indeed, many Creatives talk about regulations as apparently deliberate attempts to restrict creative work. Describing the BACC and its Codes, one Senior Creative told me that, 'they just sit in a room and try and think of reasons to stop an ad running' (Nichols). But the regulations have a more specific impact on Creatives which goes beyond a concern to provide the client with the best campaign. For all the Creatives I interviewed, one of the main negative impacts of regulation was upon the chances of UK Creatives winning advertising awards:

> We are rather hemmed in by our advertising laws in this country. They're a lot less strong in other countries which is something of a bugbear to us because we come up against them in awards and they haven't got as strict regimes as we have. I think they're over-strict in this country.
>
> (Anderson, Senior Creative)

This is clearly a major irritant for UK Creatives. Describing the prestigious 'D&AD' (Design and Art Direction) awards for creative work, another Senior Creative informed me that 'some of the ads that have won in recent years have been American ads which are free of the restrictions we've got' (Maguire). Advertising is an industry in which winning awards functions to promote an agency. But awards also offer considerable individual self-promotional leverage, translating into higher salaries and greater occupational mobility. It seems that some of the motivation behind Creatives' challenging of the regulations – and behind their rhetoric about being able to successfully flout the regulations – is this self-promotional drive. This contributes to the creation of the tension between creativity and regulation that flows through the industry. As Geoff Russell, spokesperson for the trade body the Institute of Practitioners in Advertising, told me:

> Creative people who . . . want to sail as close to the edge as they can because they want to provoke a reaction find those forms of regulation quite inhibiting. And inevitably there's going to be a sort of frisson between the regulator and the ad agency – the ad agency constantly trying to establish new frontiers and the regulating body constantly wanting to avoid either breaking rules or [provoking] public affront.
>
> (Russell, spokesperson for the IPA)

This tendency is evident in the promotional 'advertising talk' of the Creatives I interviewed. As Vicki Maguire, a Senior Creative, explained to me:

> I mean, you know, there are a lot of very highly paid people in advertising whose sole job is to 'interpret' BACC guidelines . . . if you sit down with a reel of alcohol ads then you will see that a lot of those rules have been 'interpreted', have been bent. . . . And so you play those games, but to be perfectly honest, if you've got a product that is going to be so difficult to get by the BACC you do it somewhere else – you go instore, you do it on beermats, you do it on flyposters which are illegal, but, you know. . . . There are ways and means and TV is not the be-all-and-end-all anymore. So the poor old BACC, bless their little hearts, are a bit finger-in-the-dike . . . there are so many ways around [regulation] that it's not really a big deal.
>
> (Maguire, Senior Creative)

Evidently, should the regulations on broadcast and poster advertising be considered overly restrictive, there are other options available to potential advertisers including streaming advertisements on the Internet. It is equally clear that some Creatives do not respect the regulations and actively explore ways of bending them to create what they perceive to be innovative campaigns. But this approach to advertising regulation was not shared by all the practitioners in my study. The general perception amongst Account Managers and Planners was that the shelf-life of such subversive tactics is short: 'occasionally you get people making a TV ad that's already been banned by the BACC purely so that they can get a PR hit . . . but I think the mileage from that sort of "we've taken them on" is less and less each time it happens. And each time it happens there's fewer articles going "gosh, that's shocking"' (Anonymous Account Manager). In addition, many Account Managers and Planners are highly cautious about the potential effects of producing campaigns which breach the Codes: 'you have to be very deliberate about doing that kind of thing because the repercussions are quite severe' (St Amour, Account Manager). As noted above, poster pre-vetting is considered to be a particular deterrent although few advertisers are subject to such a restriction. Claire Forbes of the Advertising Standards Authority informed me that as of January 2002, twelve companies were subject to the pre-vetting procedure in the UK. On another level, there is some scepticism about the extent to which regulations can be circumvented. One Planner told me that Account Managers' rhetoric should not be taken at face value:

> [Regulation is] an Account Management issue. And if you're an Account Manager you want to appear very cool and clever, and you suggest that you can bend [ASA and BACC codes] round your little finger. Of course that probably isn't true! . . . We aggrandise the extent to which we can affect those processes.
>
> (Southgate, Planner)

It is clear that practitioners use regulation as a site for circulating ideas about advertising and ideas about the role of different jobs in the agency. Some *talk up* the issue of flouting regulation as a means of establishing creative credibility; others take a commercially pragmatic stance and maintain that such breaching of the Codes is counter-productive. Whilst the extent to which practitioners successfully flout regulations remains unclear, it is evident that the discourses surrounding those regulations and how they might be bent are very powerful and channel multiple interests and concerns. The Institute of Practitioners in Advertising has a mandate to defend and promote advertising's profile, particularly by arguing that a system of self-regulation is effective. So the IPA considers the media attention created by controversial campaigns highly problematic:

> It gives us as a trade body quite a lot of concern because people do flout the rules, people do deliberately make use of the fact that they run something and have it judged by a regulating body and take advantage of that situation. They do cause big problems because they bring what I'll call the consumerist wing in to say that self-regulation doesn't work. Whereas of course self-regulation works for 99.99% of the advertisements that run, the ones that they never notice.
>
> (Russell, spokesperson for the IPA)

The IPA is less concerned about the number of agencies which flout the regulations or how 'successfully' they do so, but rather with the way in which advertising in general comes to be highlighted as an area that requires stricter (statutory) regulation. Thus, the primary aim of the IPA is to intervene in circuits of belief about advertising by promoting an image of the advertising industry as responsibly self-regulating.

In contrast, many regulatory bodies and pressure groups such as the anti-tobacco group ASH (Action on Smoking and Health) focus more on the impact of regulation on the sales of problematic commodities such as cigarettes. As noted in the previous chapter, tobacco manufacturers and official spokespeople for the advertising industry consistently defend cigarette advertising on the basis that it merely aims to increase market share for a brand and maintain brand loyalty rather than generate new consumers in that market. Most of the practitioners I interviewed subscribed to the general view that advertising's aims are multiple: advertising may aim to 'increase the volume sold; to increase market share; to increase penetration; to increase the rate the product is used; to reduce price sensitivity or to address specific problems of consumer perception; to arrest declining volume or share, or maintain distribution' (Davidson 1992: 37). Equally, the practitioners aligned themselves with the view that advertising's effects are multiple and that it is difficult or impossible to isolate those effects from other forms of promotion, for example, pricing, marketing or distribution. Yet there were considerable differences in how these perceptions were mobilized in relation to specific issues such as cigarette advertising.

Controversies and regulation

Practitioners' accounts of advertising controversial commodities such as tobacco and alcohol mirror the tensions existing in broader social understandings of the consumption of such products. Neither the 'truth' of advertising effects nor the 'real intentions' of practitioners' practice can be found in their accounts. But this is not due to any duplicity or intent to deceive on their part: in describing their practice and beliefs, the practitioners themselves were drawing on commonly circulating understandings of advertising, of tobacco and alcohol consumption, and of social ideals such as free choice. In describing the effects of tobacco advertising, some practitioners argued that advertising's primary role is to maintain a product's market share: 'a lot of advertising is about staying in the same place' (Sell, Account Manager). John Gregg, Global Planner for Ogilvy and Mather's British American Tobacco account, also presented this stance: 'I do honestly believe it works like that. I still don't see evidence that tobacco advertising under its current self-regulatory or government regulatory controls induces young people to smoke'. Quite apart from any judgement about the veracity of the statement – which is subject to heated debate – Gregg clearly has interests in proposing such an opinion. An Account Manager who does not work on tobacco accounts gave me a very different response when asked about the advertising and tobacco industries' claim that advertising merely aims to increase market share for a brand:

> That's bogus. They're defending it because they're defending an industry's income. It's certainly true that advertising works in lots of different ways. It's very simplistic to say that it's just about sales . . . nevertheless, a major aim

throughout lots of advertising is increasing or maintaining sales or defending them. And without a doubt, in advertising [products] such as alcohol or ciga- rettes, they want to attract new consumers – it's an essential part of maintaining their consumer base, so it's a bogus argument, I think.

(Anonymous Account Manager)

As this Account Manager notes, agencies and tobacco companies may well wish to increase overall consumption, but contrary to the implications he draws from this, it does not mean that their aim will be achieved. What is significant in the multiple accounts I was given is that there was no agreement on either the aims or the effects of advertising, particularly for products such as alcohol and tobacco. None cited data to support his or her claims but rather drew on the same multiple advertising knowledges that circulate within agencies and between agencies and clients. These knowledge-forms include advertising axioms popularized by the 'heroes' of advertising such as David Ogilvy, marketing studies, opinions in the trade press, 'commonsense' beliefs, and their own experience of the industry. Many practitioners were very self-reflexive about their knowledge practices and very aware of the contradictions of their position:

It's quite easy to sit in an ivory tower and not realise the possible effects of – not necessarily your own personal contribution – but of advertising [alcoholic] drink at all . . . Having said that, drinks brands are very important to advertising agencies, so I think there's probably an element of being a bit blinkered about it.

(Gardener, Account Director)

Other practitioners considered that promotional practices for tobacco were problematic, but displaced the blame from advertising onto marketing practices:

I do think [tobacco promotion] is worse when it's pushed towards youngsters like a lot of the cigarette manufacturers are now trying to get youngsters in Third World countries to smoke and they're doing it in a very nasty way – volleyball matches . . . I think that's very naughty. . . . But you've got the choice to smoke and you've got the choice not to smoke. I don't think an advert makes you want to smoke.

(Anderson, Senior Creative)

By shifting between a condemnation of insidious marketing practices, a defence of advertising, and an appeal to individual responsibility in our choices, this account condenses many of the tensions which circulate in the industry's practices and understandings of advertising's effects, and also in popular and governmental understandings of consumption choice. It also raises issues of individual prac- titioners' ethics. Indeed, working on tobacco accounts – although not alcohol accounts – appears to be something of a 'conscience issue' in the advertising industry. Several practitioners told me that they would not work on tobacco accounts and that there was a general understanding at agencies that you would not be required to work on such accounts if you objected to the principle. Asked why he would not work on a tobacco account, an Account Director told me:

> I've never really subscribed to the view that advertising in general is all about making people get stuff that they don't want and therefore contribute to all sorts of things like spiralling debt . . . I think it's a lot less simplistic than that but [tobacco advertising in developing countries] did seem to be the epitome of the insidious nature of advertising. That was just a line that I would have drawn. I didn't want to work on something which . . . was about contributing to the success of something which everyone knew . . . was contributing to illness.
>
> (Gardener, Account Director)

Thus on a personal level, practitioners clearly had doubts about the ethics of tobacco advertising despite simultaneously holding a belief that advertising effects on sales are neither guaranteed nor easily determined. Agencies also 'managed' ethics through certain practices: 'I think that probably a lot of agencies tend to salve their conscience a little bit by the charity work they do' (Gardener, Account Director). On a more general level, the issue is more explicitly commercial. Some agencies, such as Abbott Mead Vickers BBDO, have self-imposed bans on working on tobacco accounts and widely publicize their ethical stance. When asked why the agency had this ban, the Managing Director, Cilla Snowball, is quoted as saying, 'Because of the link with tobacco and smoking. . . . We believe tobacco advertising encourages smoking' (Palmer 2001: 23). The journalist who wrote this article in the trade paper *Marketing*, took pains to point out that Abbott Mead Vickers BBDO has held the UK Department of Health's anti-smoking account for seventeen years (ibid.). The ethics of the stance now look more like commercial pragmatics – it is common for one client to demand that an agency does not handle accounts for rival companies or companies with conflicting interests. But another practitioner I interviewed pointed out that one of the most controversial advertising and marketing practices for alcohol or cigarettes – targeting children – may not need to be so strictly policed because such tactics can be commercially counter-productive. Contrary to the general commonsense view, it may not be in a company's interests to explicitly target children in advertising campaigns:

> If you were to create a beer ad that was specifically aimed at a younger market . . . just in its tone of voice . . . you would alienate a lot of your core drinkers because they would look at as being a bit naff. . . . So you're almost shooting yourself in your foot [by aiming at children] really because you need to understand the target.
>
> (Sell, Account Manager)

From my analysis of the interviews, it is clear that some agencies and clients bend or flout the regulations, drawing considerable critical attention from the media, politicians and academics. For instance, Hastings and MacFadyen (2000b: 12) argue that the Advertising Standards Authority's self-regulatory system is not effective because tobacco manufacturers and agencies regularly flout the regulations. To support this claim they cite an agency document which discusses tobacco advertising tactics: 'stepping close to the legal rulings, this technique has proven to be very successful for Gallagher recently'. Whilst Hastings and MacFadyen take this agency account as a statement of fact – and as a statement of intent to continue bending the regulations – I would argue that the rhetoric of the agencies needs to be considered more closely in several ways. First, as demonstrated by industry surveys and the low numbers of complaints that are upheld, few agencies or client companies deliberately transgress the regulations. As I noted above, there are good commercial reasons not to engage in subversive practices. The few agencies that attempt such practices do so in order to raise their profile and enhance their image as cutting-edge practitioners, but most clients are not looking for that kind of controversial profile. This is recognized by most practitioners:

> It's certainly the case that some agencies have more of a reputation for . . . flouting and sailing close to the wind with regard to the ITC codes than others and there are some brands, some advertisers who would never even contemplate running anything which went in that direction.
>
> (Gardener, Account Director)

Second, the claims made by agencies about advertising and its effects should be viewed in the context of pressures on agencies to produce such legitimizing and competitive rhetoric. The discourses generated and circulated by agencies are part of self-promotional strategies which operate on multiple levels. For the purposes of career enhancement, individuals within agencies may exaggerate the extent to which they can successfully target specific groups, or talk up the reach of their campaigns' 'manipulative powers'. In addition, Creatives may mystify the creative process by exaggerating a campaign's persuasive potential in order to carve out a space of relative autonomy within the process of constructing a campaign and pitching it to a client. Moreover, they may aim to demonstrate their innovative techniques and individual prowess by trying to bend the regulations, or by claiming that they can. On another level, agencies pitch their talents, particularly in the UK trade magazine *Campaign*, by laying claim to innovative advertising techniques, insight, or creativity. They may even exaggerate a client's level of expenditure on a campaign in order to enhance their agency's profile, making it appear more prosperous and successful. Third, agencies engage in such self-promotional discursive practices not merely for their own commercial benefit but for the benefit of their client: in creating a media 'buzz' around a campaign for its humour, use of celebrities, or treatment of social issues (not just for controversy or breaking regulations), advertisements for that client's product are reproduced, discussed and further disseminated in press articles or television programmes. Fourth, I have argued that advertising practitioners' accounts of their beliefs, practices and intentions cannot be unambiguously framed as the site of the 'truth' about advertising. Practitioners themselves draw on, and contribute to, understandings of advertising which are widely circulating in trade bodies such as the IPA, discourses around new legislation, regulatory bodies such as the ASA and the ITC, critical accounts in the media, and in both commonsense and academic registers. Thus, examining the material from these interviews allows insights into the 'procedures of intervention' (Foucault 2001: 58) that regulation effects on advertising whilst also illuminating the ways in which practitioners attempt to intervene in the circuits of belief about advertising for commercial purposes. But the practitioners do not only attempt to direct the circuits of belief for their own ends; they actively source their own understandings of advertising effects and social impact from those very circuits which constitute what Foucault (1980: 131) has called '"political economy" of truth' of advertising.

Understanding advertising

It is clear that practitioners' views of, and beliefs in, advertising operate on multiple levels which are not founded on 'truth' as an inalienable baseline, but rather on the complex circulation of diverse understandings of advertising's form and function. These understandings, I suggest, can best be seen as 'promotional beliefs' and 'invested understandings' which apprehend advertising as an ideal rather than as a mirror or distortion of the social. Here, I am drawing on and adapting Michael Schudson's (1993) argument that advertising operates as a form of capitalist realism in which advertising does not so much represent society *as it is*, but society as it *should be* according to capitalist principles. Schudson (1993: 215) here adapts the genre of socialist realist art of the Soviet Union that was a state-sponsored, state-governed form, 'obliged to present "a correct and historically concrete representation of reality in its revolutionary development" in order to "educate the masses in the spirit of socialism"'. Stopping short of arguing that advertising is a state-governed official art-form, Schudson proposes that advertising offers the masses a lesson in the ideals of capitalism: the glorification of consumer choice, the solution to personal and social problems through consumption, material satisfaction as the ultimate individual goal. Advertising, therefore, operates by offering ideals and images of 'life and lives worth emulating' rather than by reproducing reality or mirroring the social (Schudson 1993: 215).

Schudson's account of capitalist realism can be usefully adapted to explore practitioners' invested beliefs about advertising and how these are integrated into their practice, revealing some complex understandings of 'truth' and 'reality'. As I have argued, agencies continually produce promotional rhetoric about their creative and commercial skills in order to compete with other agencies for clients' accounts. These promotional interventions operate as Foucaultian truth claims in which each agency attempts to brand research and creative skills which promise to deliver the truth of the consumer, and how to reach her, to the client. In contrast, practitioners' personal beliefs in and about advertising operate less as truth claims than as invested understandings. On a personal level, these are investments in practitioners' own sense of worth and the social responsibility of their job, as well as material investments of financial rewards and career enhancement. The practitioners do not need to 'believe in' the power of advertising – that is, they do not need to believe in any real sense of advertising's social and economic impact. Nor are they required to suspend belief in advertising, or to be sceptical about advertising's effects, for these invested understandings are not founded on any sense of advertising 'as it is'. Rather, these invested understandings operate in a register that apprehends the *ideals* of advertising. Thus as a form of capitalist realism, practitioners' understandings are based on advertising *as it should be* and not on any claim to reality *as it is*. According to these principles, advertising should be an ideal commercial form which entertains, provides information, generates profit for agencies and companies, and does not impinge on the inalienable characteristic of the free will of the individual (defined primarily as the free choice of the consumer). This is a form of capitalist realism in which the cultural intermediaries themselves are educated in the ideology of capitalism. It should not be surprising, then, that practitioners' accounts of advertising's form and function parallel those which circulate more generally and indeed draw on those common perceptions. But just because practitioners' engagement with understandings of advertising are not required to rely on belief or disbelief in any conventional sense, practitioners' accounts should not be seen as false or duplicitous. They should be seen, I propose, as 'promotional beliefs'. Here, I base my definition of promotion on Andrew Wernick's (1991: 182): promotion is 'a complex of significations which at once represents (moves in place of), advocates (moves on behalf of), and anticipates (moves ahead of) the circulating entity or entities to which it refers'. Practitioners' promotional beliefs thus *represent* and *advocate* advertising in that they are deployed as promotional resources circulating between clients and agencies and within agencies between Creatives, Planners and Account Managers. These promotional beliefs are folded together inextricably with advertising practice and function to constitute advertising as social and economic form. These beliefs *anticipate* or move ahead of advertising in that they project forward an ideal capitalist world which advertising aims to create; a world in which social ideals are articulated through consumption, consumer choice, and material satisfaction which are delivered by commercial efficiency, in turn delivering ever-increasing profit. These promotional beliefs, then, present advertising as a means of social resolution, of ordering the world according to capitalist principles. Practitioners are themselves deeply invested in these understandings whilst at the same time promoting them to clients and to a sceptical public. To reiterate, these understandings are neither 'false' nor 'true' as they do not found their discursive legitimacy on claims to truth: they project forward to ideal worlds in which advertising further extends capitalism's ideological embrace.

In this circulation of beliefs and vested interests, academic accounts of advertising do not stand in a position of detached authority, deploying analytic resources to illuminate the truth of commercial practice. Indeed, the knowledges and beliefs in advertising, commodities and consumers that are produced in advertising agencies and in academia are complexly interwoven. On a practical level, knowledge practices flow between the advertising industry and academia, confounding any sense that their forms of understanding are strictly distinct. Neither is it the case that the flow of knowledge is unidirectional: agencies and marketing practitioners borrow from academic knowledges but academia looks to advertising and marketing for confirmation of its theoretical stances. For instance, Lury and Warde (1997) argue that when market research abandoned statistical methods (which had been originally imported from academic analysis), social theory needed to elaborate a hermeneutical rather than positivistic approach to address the shift. Flowing from this, interpretative approaches in academia gained prominence, installing 'culture' as the key object of analysis. Analytic approaches such as that of 'lifestyle' consumption which developed in the advertising and marketing industries (with the aid of understandings borrowed from academia), then became reincorporated into academic analyses as confirmation of academia's original premises: 'theory seems to be reappropriating models of behaviour that were the consequence of the practical application for marketing purposes of techniques that social science originally exported' (Lury and Warde 1997: 101). In this move, social theory (unreflexively) comes to reform the social world in the image and language of the lifestyle advertisement. So advertising practitioners attempt to lend legitimacy to their practices by using techniques shared with academic analysis, for example, focus groups or semiotic analysis. And at the same time, academics attempt to map the social world using 'second hand' academic techniques and ideas which have been adapted by advertising and marketing practitioners for their own purposes and are now employed by academia as evidence of the applicability of their theories to the 'real world'. In this way, 'the critic and advertiser are locked into endlessly reworking each other's methods in complementary idioms' (Davidson 1992: 175).

This mutual articulation of knowledges implicates academic analyses firmly in the circuits of belief in and about advertising. Such a recognition should, I believe, inspire academic accounts to temper their more programmatic critiques with a reflexive awareness of the forms of knowledge that are produced about and *through* advertising as a cipher. Critiques of such academic analyses abound in the advertising industry. Here, Geoff Russell of the Institute of Practitioners in Advertising identifies what he calls 'consumerists' – those who aim to champion consumer rights but misunderstand the nature of advertising and consumer choice – as the prime culprits:

> [Consumerists] do attract a certain type of person – middle class, polytechnic lecturer – who has a view that they themselves, of course, can understand these things. What they have to do is protect those people who can't. It's therefore their job to go out and say . . . that advertising is creating desires rather than needs, promoting discontent.
>
> (Russell, spokesperson for the IPA)

Whilst a rather sweeping criticism, this account touches on an important characteristic of cultural analysis which often sees 'lecturers in communication studies pummelling, dismembering and pouring polysyllabic scorn on this louche opiate of our times' (Davidson 1992: 1). Throughout this and the previous chapter, I have argued that advertising is constituted as text, as competitive business, as economic nexus, and as socio-cultural form through the circulation of multiple understandings of advertising's form and function. A thorough analysis of advertising must attend to this diversity of form and function and must address how the flow of beliefs about advertising actively constitutes advertising. I hope that my approach may go some way towards understanding advertising and the range of criticisms that are levelled at it. For instance, practitioners I interviewed suggested that the degree of criticism directed at advertising results in part from the way agencies' own promotional rhetoric frames advertising as a target for those concerns: 'we have set ourselves up as these manipulative masters . . . we talk very much about our role in popular culture. We set ourselves up as terribly influential so we ask to be criticized' (Southgate, Account Planner). The self-promotional circulation of claims about advertising's effects rebounds and attracts intensified criticism and regulation. This is certainly borne out in the example of Hastings and MacFadyen's (2000a, 2000b) research which I discussed in this and the previous chapter. In their analysis of agency documents about tobacco accounts, they took agencies' claims of manipulative prowess at face value and produced highly critical reports which were cited as evidence of advertising's power in the consultation document of the Tobacco Advertising and Promotion Bill (Department of Health 2002). This circular logic or self-fulfilling prophecy also appears to be an important factor in constantly re-figuring advertising both as focus of criticism and as a news story. Claire Forbes of the Advertising Standards Authority, highlighted advertising's good 'news value' and hence its high media profile:

> [Advertising's] very fast moving – it's changing all the time which is always good from a news point of view. You don't want something which is static. . . . It's seen as being at the forefront of trends, it's seen as being glamorous and trendy and that all, kind of, adds to its attractiveness to the media.
>
> (Forbes, ASA)

Its appeal to the media ensures a heightened public profile for advertising and this increased visibility in the media, in turn, may be taken as further evidence of advertising's ubiquity and hence effectiveness. Advertising's power may, ironically, be read off from the high number of media accounts that reproduce certain advertisements and subject advertising to critical scrutiny.

These circuits of belief do not reproduce and disseminate 'falsehoods' about advertising nor are they merely immaterial circulations of 'advertising talk': they intervene in the political economy of truth about advertising and have material effects. For instance, the understandings circulating in policy and legislative documents I analysed in the previous chapter may have unintended, material effects. Banning tobacco advertising will leave tobacco companies severely restricted avenues for promoting their cigarette brands and debates in the advertising and marketing trade press have suggested that companies may respond by competitive price-cutting. As cutting the price of commodities has long been deployed as a means of very successfully increasing their consumption, the advertising ban may paradoxically contribute to an increase in cigarette consumption. As I suggested in the previous chapter, such restrictions may also have the unforeseen effect of producing more imaginative promotional practices, as one Planner notes: 'if anything [regulation has] forced the industry [in the UK] to be sharper and more creative' (Gregg). To take another example, the high profile of advertising and its popular perception as manipulative ensures that it is prime material for channelling party political concerns and for scoring political points. As one Account Manager argued, 'in the last ten years I think advertising generally has become more distrusted and more suspect in a wider debate. It's related, I think, to the same kind of cynicism there is about spin or about focus groups or anything that's perceived as manipulative' (Anonymous). A Senior Creative pushed this analysis further,

> Over the past five years, especially with the Labour Party . . . words associated with advertising such as 'spin', the obviously rebranding of new institutions such as New Labour . . . all those things which are seen as advertising tools have been shamelessly laid bare. . . . I think that we are going to get a bit of stick [from the government] because Labour won't want to be seen as facile as most of us in the advertising industry are, so they're going to come down on the side of 'we'll ban this' and 'we're looking at this' . . . just to save face.
>
> (Maguire, Senior Creative)

In this way, generalized perceptions about advertising can be discursively mobilized for political, promotional motives and can have material effects such as the introduction of regulation.

Most striking in these flows of knowledge is the way in which advertising practitioners reincorporate elements of the circuits of belief into their own understandings. The same Creative cited above – who in every other respect demonstrated a scepticism about the commercial power of advertising and an awareness of political imperatives – simultaneously drew on the discourses of advertising's effectiveness which circulate in policy and legislative arenas. In an interesting inversion, she says of advertising: 'when it's right, it's powerful. It must be, or else they wouldn't be trying to ban [tobacco] advertising' (Maguire, Senior Creative). Here, beliefs about advertising's power which are generated across the multiple sites of trade associations, self-regulatory bodies, legislative initiatives, academic analyses, and 'commonsense' understandings, come full circle and are reincorporated into practitioners' own repertoires of belief about advertising, only then to be condensed and recirculated as 'proofs' of advertising's power. Andrew Wernick (1991: 15) has argued that advertising is part of a promotional matrix of design and production based on 'artificial semiosis: the industrial manufacture of meaning and myth'. But I am arguing here that advertising does not merely generate seductive myths about products; advertising is itself a myth which circulates through various domains and multiple registers, functioning as a currency or lightening rod for a range of social concerns. Amongst the various commercial interests it channels, advertising also functions for academics and for regulators as an index of the social or a kind of 'myth' in Barthes' (1974) sense. For regulators, it appears to offer a way of controlling social practices, especially 'dangerous consumption practices' such as smoking; hence the idea that banning tobacco advertising will be an efficient means of social engineering – effectively altering people's behaviour. For many academics, it appears to offer a convenient means of making 'the social' or 'the cultural' available to analysis; for instance, advertising is often used as a cultural indicator or kind of litmus test in which characteristics of society are read off from advertisements themselves or from the imagined power of the advertising industry. I have argued here that such accounts need to take a much more nuanced approach and need to recognize academic analyses' own implication in the circulation of understandings of advertising. I have also argued that advertising myths do not merely circulate *within* a commercial context; they actively contribute to *constituting* that context. In parallel, advertising practitioners should not be considered merely as 'cultural intermediaries' in the classic sense of providing symbolic goods and services, mediating between distinct social registers, and mediating the relationship between consumers and commodities (see Bourdieu 2000). In fact, practitioners attempt to institute systems or currencies of commercial exchange based on their purported skills and are thus active in constituting arenas of exchange rather than simply mediating between those that are already established. In the next chapter, I extend this analysis to explore how these advertising myths coalesce around the advertising text itself and the anxieties and controversies that are articulated in advertising for 'dangerous commodities' such as tobacco and alcohol.

4 Animating images
Advertisements, texts, commodities

Certain pivotal accounts of consumer society posit that objects are now the index or the defining mark of the contemporary field. Jean Baudrillard (1988: 29) has argued, 'we are living the period of objects: that is, we live by their rhythm, according to their incessant cycles'. For him, this shift in relationality between persons and things is so elemental that it constitutes 'a fundamental mutation in the ecology of the human species' (ibid.). Other classic accounts figure contemporary consumer capitalism as oriented around – and defined through – images. For Guy Debord (1994 [1967]), this is a society of the spectacle in which 'the spectacle is *capital* accumulated to the point where it becomes image' (1994: 24, emphasis in original). Hence, spectacle is more than a mere a collection of images; it is 'a social relationship between people that is mediated by images' (Debord 1994: 12). This emphasis on the image, and on a teleological shift towards a society increasingly mediated by the visual, is often framed in contemporary analyses by a narrative of loss. Materiality is given over or lost to the image, the sign, the brand; the emphasis in social practices shifts from production to consumption; the commodity as material form loses its impact upon society as the significance of images and signs rises exponentially (for example, see Jhally 1987). In parallel, there is an assumed destabilization of commodities as unambiguously bounded, defined objects, and a redefinition of consumer needs (Leiss *et al.* 1990). Needs become fragmented 'in reciprocal relation to the disintegration of goods as determinate objects. Many mass-produced goods are now temporary associations of physical and imputed characteristics'(ibid.: 70). This understanding of the disaggregation of objects has been taken up more recently by Lash and Urry (1994: 4) who argue that '[objects] are progressively emptied of material content. What is increasingly produced are not material objects, but *signs*'. This analysis figures the erosion of the significance of materiality and the proportionate augmentation of the role of the visual in distributing value through the circulation of signs.

In alternative accounts, the significance of images and objects – and particularly advertisements and commodities – resides in their complex interrelationship rather than in any zero-sum attribution of prominence. Anthropological analyses have developed this perspective most fully; for instance, Sahlins (1976: 178) argues that 'the cultural order is realised . . . as an order of goods. . . . The goods stand as an object code for signification and valuation of persons and occasions, functions and situations'. Here, objects mediate and give form to the social world of humans. Similarly, Douglas and Isherwood (1979: 14) argue that goods do not function merely as discrete messages but rather constitute an entire 'information system': they communicate information but also form the very framework that classifies persons and events. This is an understanding of commodities as 'material–symbolic entities' (Leiss 1978: 84) in which the emphasis is not exclusively placed on the practical *use* of such objects, or on their role as visual symbols of social values or structure, but also encompasses the discursive constitution of the relationship between persons and things, things and images.

Other accounts focus solely on commodities, offering nuanced perspectives on the processes of categorization of 'the commodity' and 'the thing'. Arjun Appadurai's (1986) well-known analysis does not figure a pre-constituted commodity that circulates in social and economic relations of exchange. For Appadurai, the commodity is not defined by any specificity of its materiality or method of production; the commodity is a category through which things pass, altering their status and value in the process. He does not presume the specificities of what should count as a commodity and his question is not, 'what is a commodity?', but rather, 'what sort of exchange is commodity exchange?' (Appadurai 1986: 9). With this focus, he aims to explore the trajectories that things take into and out of commodity status.

> I propose that *the commodity situation in the social life of any 'thing' be defined as the situation in which its exchangeability (past, present, or future) for some other thing is its socially relevant feature.* Further, the commodity situation, defined in this way, can be disaggregated into: (1) the commodity phase of the social life of any thing; (2) the commodity candidacy of any thing; and (3) the commodity context in which any thing may be placed.
>
> (Appadurai 1986: 13, emphasis in original)

In this analysis, commodities are closely related to things or objects, but are not co-extensive with them; things can become commodities, and things can move out of commodity status. In addition, there are different categories of commodity: commodities 'by destination' (those intended for exchange by their producers); commodities 'by metamorphosis' (things not originally intended for commodity status); commodities 'by diversion' (objects which are placed in commodity status but which were originally protected from it); and 'ex-commodities' (things no longer in a commodity state) (Appadurai 1986: 16). This multifaceted framework aims to account for the social life of things – their mutability and mobility – in contrast to analyses that presume a fixed category of 'commodity' to which things either belong or are excluded from.

In Appadurai's account, things are important because they can be made to speak about human relations: the trajectories of things can be analysed to reveal, 'the human transactions and calculations that enliven things' (Appadurai 1986: 5). Things and commodities are here figured primarily as resources for symbolic analysis – they mutely embody social values in their circulation and can thus function as privileged entry points for analysis of the social: 'things-in-motion . . . illuminate their human and social context' (ibid.). It is certainly the case that analysing objects can reveal much about the social and historical context in which they circulate. But such an analysis risks overlooking the relationship between the constitution of the classifications of 'thing' and 'person' in that very circulation. In the same volume, Igor Kopytoff (1986: 66) argues for an approach that focuses on the 'career' of a thing. He calls this a 'cultural biography of things' that tracks a thing's constitution and reconstitution in culturally and historically specific contexts (ibid.). Such an analysis of things would pose a series of biographical questions such as:

> What, sociologically, are the biographical possibilities inherent in its 'status' and in the period and culture, and how are these possibilities realized? Where does the thing come from and who made it? What has been its career so far, and what do people consider an ideal career for such things? What are the recognized 'ages' or periods in a thing's 'life', and what are the cultural markers for them? How does a thing's use change with age, and what happens to it when it reaches the end of its usefulness?
>
> (Kopytoff 1986: 66–7)

In parallel to Appadurai's approach, this analysis focuses on the cultural construction of things and the way in which they are classified and reclassified *as things* – as well as specific categories of thing – as they circulate spatially and temporally. Significantly, Kopytoff does not cast a thing as the base materiality that functions as an anchorage point from which the category 'commodity' may be constructed and maintained. Neither do things function merely as carriers for cultural signification. Certainly, things are attributed social meaning and may be analysed to reveal the values and ideals of a particular society. But for Kopytoff, things are more than dumb bearers of cultural meaning or indicators of modes of social exchange: things are implicated in the very constitution of the category 'person' such that, 'one can draw an analogy between the way societies construct individuals and the way they construct things' (Kopytoff 1986: 89).

This chapter focuses on this strand of analysis. I explore how the force of criticisms about advertising and consumer culture partially resides in the tension between the categories of things, images and persons. The field of consumption and advertising is broad and encompasses a wide range of analytic issues and political concerns – I am not suggesting that the processes of categorization of 'person' and 'thing' that advertising articulates is the only or even the primary element of significance. It is, however, an important area that deserves more critical attention. As I outlined in Chapter 1, specific demarcations in the classifications of person and thing co-articulated with capitalist expansion in the nineteenth century (see Seltzer 1992). In this chapter, I track one element of this theme, arguing that an important factor in commodity exchange is the traffic in the terms of 'person' and 'thing'. This is a flow of capital and materialities, but is also a flow of communication, information and sign-values. The focus here is the forms of relationality between advertising and what have come to be seen as 'dangerous commodities' such as tobacco and alcohol. It is in these sites that the regulative drive to delimit and secure the boundaries of advertisements, commodities, and persons is most evident and thus most available to analysis. Following on from my account in Chapter 2, I examine how advertising as a representational form *itself* comes to be pathologized. Here, I argue that contemporary tobacco and alcohol advertisements most forcefully highlight and draw critical attention to a particular form of relationality between advertising images and commodities, but they are not the sole cause of advertising's negative or dangerous image. I argue that contemporary discourses in Euro-American societies articulate a particular form of relationality that intensifies an already-existent tendency to locate pathology at the level of representation, and particularly in advertising images. As outlined in Chapter 3, circuits of belief in advertising are generated that are not reliant on material 'proofs' of advertising's effects, and as a corollary, these circuits reproduce and intensify a sense that advertising is pathological. This, in turn, makes objects appear less stable as they are thought to be increasingly susceptible to the supposedly intensified powers of (advertising) images. This, I suggest, is part of a perceived crisis in consumer culture that is articulated as a crisis of agency in debates over addiction and compulsive shopping. It is also, as I go on to argue, a broad regulatory imperative articulating a sense of crisis in the ownership of the relation between reality and representation, freedom and determination, life and death.

Text, commodity, pathology

Advertising is one part of a process of stabilization and destabilization of flows of beliefs, materialities and values into the commodity-form. Organized by, but by no means determined by advertising practitioners, its textual form provisionally freezes a moment of those flows and makes legible certain values. Throughout this chapter I will argue that advertising should not be considered a privileged site in this constellation of formations: we should not imagine that through close textual analysis it will yield its essence or the secrets of its commercial persuasion. As I suggested in Chapters 2 and 3, advertising is not the culmination or endpoint of various processes of branding, research, and marketing: it is a temporary stabilization of a flow of beliefs and commercial values into a representation form. I demonstrated in Chapter 2 how the regulatory codes produced by the Advertising Standards Authority do indeed figure the text of the advertisement as the privileged moment in the promotion of consumption and primary causal factor in influencing (undesirable) behaviour. In the enforcement of the regulatory codes, the ASA acts to pathologize advertising as a representational form through the textual analysis they perform on advertisements, specifically locating pathology at the level of the text. This is a textual zero-sum game whereby the imperatives of the ASA – to locate and regulate 'dangerous' or offensive advertisements – must be addressed in the terms of reference available to it. The ASA only has power over the textual content of advertisements and it cannot, for example, regulate which commodities may or may not be advertised. To address its regulatory imperatives, the ASA thus retreats to the level of text and produces detailed descriptive analyses of specific advertisements on which they base generalized claims about the texts' effects on viewers. This functions to substantialize or animate advertising, at once attributing it a form of agency and erasing viewers' agency in their imagined collapse to the persuasian of the text.

The analysis that follows attempts to avoid this conceptual dead-end by considering advertisements as temporary stabilizations of multiple processes. These provisional stabilizations function on the level of the individual text (that is, a collection of image, text and form of address that makes the representational form legible as an advertisement) and on the general level of advertising as a cultural form (for just as commodities are stabilized into legible materialities, advertising as a specific textual form with specific effects is stabilized). These stabilizations include a coalescence of beliefs in and about advertising: those of the advertising practitioners; those of the regulators that inform what is acceptable or unacceptable in an advertisement; those of the viewer; those which focus more generally on the power of images. Hence the specific themes mobilized in advertisements may not be significant in their own right, but neither are they arbitrary. Their significance lies in their form of relationality to other cultural formations, that is, in the *way* in which they connect or articulate with them. Therefore, contrary to many beliefs and practices such as those of the ASA, the specific textual content of an advertisement is neither the sole element nor the locus of the power of that advertisement; it should not be the primary point of intervention for those who wish to regulate advertising and consumption, nor privileged point of analysis for the critic. In the following section, I focus on how certain forms of relationality anchor the product and text in their articulation of themes and modes of address, thus enabling a moment of stabilization. But the success of a theme or mode of address in anchoring a campaign does not necessarily translate into increased sales of the product, increased profile (for product, company or advertising agency), or into creative awards for the advertising agency.

I have analysed elsewhere how humour and especially irony is often used in advertising as a distancing device (Cronin 2000a). In the context of tobacco and alcohol advertising, humour is employed as a way of accessing and re-presenting discourses around 'dangerous' commodities or forms of consumption. This is achieved in one way by explicitly referencing and playing with the very codes of compulsion or addiction that mark such advertising as dangerous.[1] In an advertisement for Absolut vodka (Figure 4.1), the characteristic outlining of the vodka bottle shape (that is repeated in various forms throughout the long-running campaign) is here formed by a collection of training shoes and the strap-line 'Absolut obsession'. The collection of shoes is neatly arranged and presented as a kind of taxonomy of that particular commodity: a wide array of styles and colours are displayed by, and to, the consumer/owner. The series of Absolut advertisements does not rely on addiction or compulsion as its textual anchoring theme. But the visual citing of shopping compulsion or addiction in this advertisement makes explicit that which is implicit in advertising as a cultural form – that the contemporary dominant form of relationality between commodities and persons,

Figure 4.1 Absolut vodka advertisement, 'Absolut obsession' (with permission from V&S Vin & Sprit AB. ABSOLUT COUNTRY OF SWEDEN VODKA & LOGO, ABSOLUT, ABSOLUT BOTTLE DESIGN AND ABSOLUT CALLIGRAPHY ARE TRADEMARKS OWNED BY V&S VIN & SPRIT AB.© 2002 V&S VIN & SPRIT AB)

advertisements and commodities, and advertisements and persons is figured in many registers as dangerous and sometimes pathological. In the Absolut advertisement, the popular discourse of compulsive shopping and the display of commodities and its associated pleasures are deployed as promotion for what is generally seen as a potentially dangerous form of consumption – drinking alcohol. This is an ironic transference of significance across different commodities via the form of advertising: potential addiction to a *substance* (alcohol) is here humorously elided by its connection with the idea of consuming obsessions or addiction to certain *practices* (shopping and collecting).

The themes of compulsive shopping, and its metonymical referencing of alcohol consumption deployed in the advertisement, make evident a form of relationality between what we apprehend as substances (and their relatives: things and objects) and practices. In contemporary discourses, substances or objects on the one hand, and practices on the other, are generally held in a tension with one another and hence kept apart on a conceptual level. A practice such as shopping requires as its reference point an animating force in the form of a human actor. Thus in citing the theme of shopping, the category of person is invoked, yet this category of person must be keep distinct from that of object or substance (such as alcohol). Bruno Latour (1993: 11) calls this process a 'purification' in which humans and non-humans are constantly defined as distinct, impermeable categories. But by mobilizing themes of compulsion or addiction in its reference to compulsive or obsessive shopping, the advertisement breaches those distinctions between person and object in figuring their pathological merging or collapsing together. Indeed, in many key discourses of addiction and in the regulatory codes for alcohol and tobacco advertising, there can be traced an over-arching concern with maintaining the perceived correct or healthy distance between the consuming self and the commodity, and between the advertising image and the substance or commodity. As outlined in Chapter 2, addictive compulsion is framed in regulatory codes, government bills and by health promotion organizations as the collapse of the subject's agency into the substance or commodity. A corollary of this framing is the de-humanizing of the subject, now bereft of agency or in possession of a contaminated agency, and the related animation of the substance or commodity: commodities such as alcohol are thus thought to act upon the subject, confiscating their agency and identity, and replacing them with the identity of 'addict' and impoverished acts directed by compulsion. This intermingling between persons and objects is what Latour (1993: 11) calls a process of 'translation' and what Haraway (1991: 215) calls a multitude of 'illicit fusions'. This produces mixtures or hybrids of the very categories whose impermeable distinction has been so strongly shored up and defended.[2] Furthermore, the notion (and indeed fear) of these person–object hybrids relies upon a prior (unarticulated, implicit) under-standing that those very categories are not as perfectly distinct and unbreachable as we may publicly articulate. It is this tacit recognition of the translation between categories, Latour argues, that makes the notion of purification possible. Hence, the mingling of person and object or substance that compulsive shopping or alcohol addiction conjures up so vividly already has a powerful discursive purchase in the very way we figure the distinction between person and object. The shoes in the Absolut advertisement that become pathologically animated or 'humanized' in their implication in compulsive practices can only be considered so if there were a prior (tacit, barely legible) understanding of their intimate, animate relation to the category of person. As I argued in Chapter 1, this relation is historically and culturally specific and functions as a powerful nexus through which conceptualizations of personhood are worked through and articulated. The recognition of the relationships between the categories of person and thing is not generally voiced or publicly rehearsed and this denial of relationality leads to a proliferation of precisely that which society wishes to erase: as Latour (1993: 12) notes, 'the more we forbid ourselves to conceive of hybrids, the more possible their interbreeding becomes'. So, paradoxically, the forceful investment in the belief that commodities are inanimate, non-agentic objects effectively animates them, restating and fuelling the circuits of belief in particular effects of consumption (such as compulsion or addiction). The advertisement provisionally freezes all these understandings and restates the conceptual polarity and impermeability of the person–thing nexus: in representing the relations between commodities, persons and images, advertising acts to constitute the divisions between those categories. At the same time, the act of division animates the very relationality and interdependence of those categories that it seeks to erase. Law and Benschop articulate this representational work or labour of division:

> To represent is to perform division. To represent is to generate distributions. . . . It is to perform, or to refuse to perform, a world of spatial assumptions populated by subjects and objects. To represent thus renders other possibilities impossible, unimaginable. It is, in other words, to perform a politics.
>
> (Law and Benschop 1997: 158)

Advertisements thus perform distinctions between objects and persons. This act of division functions to delimit and constitute the classification of person. At the same time, advertisements perform momentary stabilizations of a range of commercial processes and circuits of beliefs in and about advertising. Advertisements should not be accorded privileged status in analyses of promotion or cultural change as their significance lies not in any essence they could be attributed, but in their form of relationality to commodities, commercial practices and beliefs, and to practices of consumers. Yet many contemporary understandings do indeed frame advertising as a special cultural form and as a key driving force in people's behaviour. As I will elaborate, it is the potential merging or collapsing of that which must be kept distinct – commodities and persons, images and substances, subjects and representation – that generates so much anxiety about, and criticism of, advertising. These distinctions are rehearsed in regulations, debates about advertising, and in advertisements themselves and are often framed in terms of disease, risk and death alongside addiction and compulsion.

In the context of the restrictions placed on advertising by regulatory codes, in order to gain some kind of representational purchase or impact, the advertisements frequently feed into or push against the very concepts of danger, disease, addiction and ill-health that they are accused of fostering. One campaign that has become very well known for this trend in the UK is that of the Gallaher-owned brand of cigarettes, Silk Cut. This long-running campaign uses the signifiers of purple silk and various images related to cutting, thus representing the colour of the cigarette pack and the brand name. In one Silk Cut advertisement (Figure 4.2), a razor blade is suspended in a block of ice along with a strip of purple silk. The compulsory health warning at the foot of the image is displayed prominently: 'smoking causes fatal diseases'. In another (Figure 4.3), a surreal image of a woman is figured with a maniacal grin cutting her finger nails with a range of sharp, deadly looking knives, axes, saws and scissors spread out before her on a purple background. Again, the health warning, 'smoking kills', is prominently displayed as the regulations require. Both advertisements negotiate the strict regulatory codes for tobacco advertising by producing a textual address that is abstracted from any obvious references to smoking. As examined in Chapter 2, before tobacco advertising was banned in the UK (as of 14 February 2003), the codes prohibited tobacco advertisements from attaching positive associations to tobacco or to the practice of smoking. For example:

> Smoking should not be associated with social, sexual, romantic or business success and advertisements should not be sexually titillating, though the choice of brand may be linked to taste or discernment. In particular, advertisements should not link smoking with people who are evidently wealthy, fashionable, sophisticated or successful or who possess other attributes or qualities that may reasonably be expected to command admiration or encourage emulation.
>
> (Advertising Standards Authority 2000a, Code 66.19)

In addition, 'advertisements should not contain actual or implied testimonials or endorsements from well-known people, famous fictitious characters or people doing jobs or occupying positions which are generally regarded as admirable' (ASA Code 66.20). There are many other codes dealing with specificities such as prohibiting the use of models who are, or who look, under the age of twenty-five. Faced with these detailed restrictions, and driven by an imperative to produce striking promotional texts, the advertisements precisely invert the promotional line taken by most advertising. Advertising generally operates in a positive register, offering images of well-being (Falk 1997; Leiss *et al.* 1990). In contrast, a significant number of tobacco and alcohol advertisements explicitly reference and play with 'dangerous' codes. By using references to cutting, the Silk Cut advertisements indicate their brand name but also draw on negative themes of danger, risk, and potential violence in an ironic form of address. These themes of danger and risk create a consonance with the compulsory health warnings which provide unambiguous commentaries on the consumption practice being promoted: in these two advertisements the warnings read, 'smoking causes fatal diseases' and 'smoking kills'. In this way, the advertisements mobilize established and widely circulating

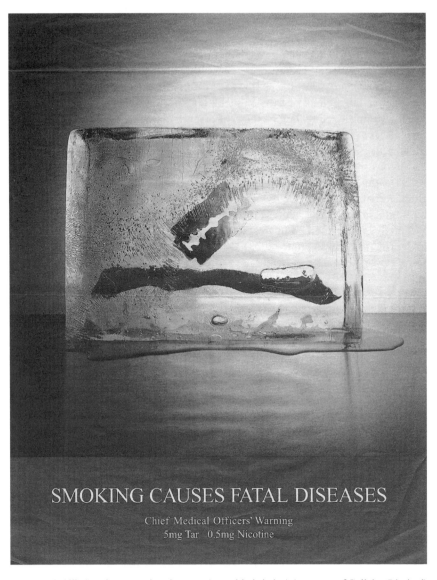

Figure 4.2 Silk Cut cigarette advertisement (razor blade in ice) (courtesy of Gallaher Limited)

Figure 4.3 Silk Cut cigarette advertisement (knives and blades) (courtesy of Gallaher Limited)

understandings that smoking is a dangerous consumption practice that can produce potentially fatal conditions such as cancer.

The codes used in these advertisements are drawn from historically and culturally specific notions of disease, death, and in parallel, ideas of what it means to live. Foucault has famously argued that conceptions of death shifted radically in nineteenth-century Europe such that death detached itself from counter-nature and became '*embodied* in the *living bodies* of individuals' (Foucault 2000a: 196, emphasis in original). Death comes to be thought *of* us and *within* us rather than as a force external to humanity. Hence we carry our deaths within us and indeed it is this very perception that feeds a sense of ourselves as individuals, living unique lives and facing unique, individual deaths. According to Foucault, this interior-ization and individualization of death stands in contrast to Renaissance conceptions of death as the great leveller, universalizing all in its sweep and eradicating differences of rank or fortune:

> Now, on the contrary, it is constitutive of singularity; it is in that perception of death that the individual finds himself, escaping from a monotonous, average life; in the slow, half-subterranean, but already visible approach of death, the dull, common life becomes an individuality at last; a black border isolates it and gives it the style of its own truth.
>
> (Foucault 2000a: 171)

For Foucault, the sense of our own inevitable death functions to delimit and also individuate our lives as unique expressions of self in our personally-inflected styles of mortality. The reflexive awareness of the death that we can name as our own lends a rather heroic aura to our otherwise unremarkable existence. What is particularly significant for my argument is that, on a broader scale, the discourse of reflexive mortality functions as the ultimate 'black-boxing' of the human as type or classi-fication. Just as marketing and advertising practitioners attempt to name, delimit or 'black-box' groups of consumers in order to target them, the discourse of a unique human self-awareness pivoting on our mortality functions to isolate humans as distinct from animals and things.

The effects of such discourses are multiple. In a contemporary Euro-American context, I would argue that death discursively stabilizes or substantializes the category of 'the person' as an individuated subject and as distinct from the category 'thing'. One way this is secured is by drawing a distinction between the finite social life of a human and the potentially infinite social life of a thing.[3] I am arguing that the contemporary form of relationality between commodities, things and persons draws on these terms and rehearses the tensions in, and anxieties about, keeping the categories distinct. Hence the discursive force of the Silk Cut advertisements (Figures 4.2 and 4.3) does not lie straightforwardly in their deployment of striking images that allude to risk, danger and death. Where the advertisements derive their impact is in their forceful restating of the potential blurring of discursive distinctions or relations between persons and commodities, advertisements and persons, reality and representation. By promoting cigarettes and referencing risk, the advertisements implicitly derive their discursive consistency from understandings of dangerous forms of consumption (including potential addiction) and how they are imagined to stage a fracturing of the boundary between the self and the commodity. As noted above, regulatory bodies and many political and academic accounts figure addiction as the collapse of agency or willpower and the threat of a pathological merging of person and drug, person and alcohol, person and commodity. Many of the long series of Silk Cut advertisements tap into and play on this tension by presenting a range of objects in ways which lend them a peculiarly animated aura and seem to attribute to each a sinister will of its own. In many of the advertisements not illustrated here, sharp objects, plants and various icons appear to come alive and lead animated existences that are cut loose from the human world – they are literally abstracted from humans and human referents and lead social lives that have their own (often menacing) purposes. Whilst the dangers of smoking are elided and unreferenced in any explicit way, the objects appear to promise risk and danger both through the theme of cutting, slicing and piercing, and through their breaching of the subject–object dichotomy in their newly animated state. The risks promised by the textual address are compounded by the perception that advertising as a cultural form dangerously erodes or even collapses the distinctions between images and the person in working its persuasive influence. As I argued in the previous chapter, advertising is thought to impinge upon the sacrosanct boundaries of the person and influence or direct their actions. This concern is played out in various forms but is most evident in anxieties about consuming behaviours such smoking or drinking alcohol.

My concern at this point is to outline how political, media and academic debates constantly rehearse the discursive distinctions between persons and objects, objects and commodities, advertising images and individuals' behaviour, reality and representation, and focus anxieties on the involution of these categories. The staging of these relations occurs across multiple sites including that of counter-cultural groups. The Canada-based group called Adbusters is one of the most well-known creators of images which satirize advertising. The group produces a website and a monthly magazine called *Adbusters: The Journal of the Mental Environment* and aims to reveal what it casts as the brute truths of consumer culture and the realities behind glossy advertising.[4] One of its tactics is the creation of what the group calls 'spoof ads'. These ads subvert conventional advertising campaigns by parodying their conventions and re-encoding their messages to challenge – as Adbusters perceives it – the way advertising distorts the truths of consumption. In a satire on Absolut vodka advertisements (Figure 4.4), the tag-line 'absolute silence' mimics the pithy Absolut slogans which run throughout its campaigns (see Figure 4.1). The coffin-image of the Adbusters' satire echoes the characteristic bottle-shape reproduced throughout the Absolut campaigns. The absolute endpoint of vodka consumption, the spoof advertisement appears to tell us, is death. This is an attempt to demystify the representational sophistry of advertising and to unveil the realities of the consumption of certain commodities. Another Adbusters' image, 'Marlboro Country' (Figure 4.5), plays on Marlboro cigarette advertisements and is similar in its aims. It resituates the well-known Marlboro horse, now riderless,

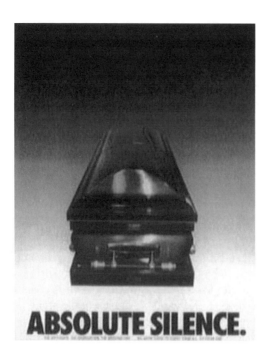

Figure 4.4 Adbusters spoof advertisement, 'Absolute silence' (courtesy of Adbusters)

Figure 4.5 Adbusters spoof advertisement, 'Marlboro country' (courtesy of Adbusters)

in a graveyard rather than in the ruggedly romantic landscape of the 'Wild West' so strongly associated with Marlboro advertisements. Again, the aim is to peel away the gloss of the Marlboro advertisements and reveal the truth of cigarette consumption that, for Adbusters, is located in disease and death. A key presumption that underlies Adbusters' approach is a belief in the power of advertising images to influence people's behaviour. But what is more sinister, is that this influence is implicitly framed as an unhealthy encroaching of the representational form into the boundaries of the subject, or as an attempt to reroute or compromise the self's agency. It is imagined to have a corrosive effect on the agency of the self such that the subsequent consumption of the commodity collapses the clear distinction between person and substance in (forms of addictive or compulsive) consumption. This, together with the disease and death that is presumed to follow, is the reality that advertising as representation is thought to obscure. Hence, 'anti-advertisements' or 'subverts' operate the same representational logic as advertising campaigns not only in their tactical, subversive referencing of advertising's conventions and codes: they gain their discursive charge through drawing on the same form of relationality between persons and objects, reality and representation as advertising itself. For this reason, Adbusters' drive for demystification, and indeed the health warnings on cigarette advertisements and packets, may not have the intended impact. Drawing on Foucault's (2000a) analysis of mortality and self-reflexivity, it is possible to argue that such warnings about the consumption-related realities of disease and death may, contrary to intention, positively reinforce smoking and drinking behaviours by highlighting a sense of individuality. The black border of finitude that circumscribes a life gives it meaning and individuality: the perception of a death which is uniquely our own lends a particularity to our life (ibid.). In this context, the threat of death as a result of our individual consumption choices does not necessarily strike a note of dread. On the contrary, such a threat may revalidate a sense of ourselves as individual through our consumption practices – our unique styles of mortality.

This individualized sense of being and personal choice is a key form of textual address in tobacco and alcohol advertising. A Drum rolling tobacco advertisement (Figure 4.6) features a masculine hand, a hand-rolled cigarette and the tag-line, 'It's in your hands. ✓ Made the right choice in roll-ups anyway'. The address plays on the theme of choice: a tick next to the cigarette validates the consumer's choice in tobacco, whilst a cross next to the mark left by an absent wedding ring invalidates that particular choice. The intended humour of the advertisement draws its force from the discourses that frames life choices as expressions of a sense of individuality. The choice to smoke, and hence to risk the dangers clearly indicated by health warnings, feeds into cultural understandings that our unique death marks our life as unique: our 'dangerous' consumption choices articulate the black border that delimits our life-span and hence produces a sense of ourselves as individual. The address of the Drum advertisement aims to deflect any anxieties about a potential (pathological) breaching of the border between self and substance (tobacco) by channelling that very sense of risk through an enactment of individuality. In contrast, one aim of Adbusters' satirical 'spoof-ads' is to highlight

PROTECT CHILDREN: DON'T MAKE
THEM BREATHE YOUR SMOKE

Chief Medical Officers' Warning

Figure 4.6 Drum tobacco advertisement, 'It's in your hands' (courtesy of Imperial Tobacco Limited)

what they see as corporate responsibility for contemporary consumption ills. Many of their campaigns target specific companies or brands such as Marlboro, and emphasize corporate responsibility for promoting unhealthy practices. Yet this approach may fail to hit home as it runs counter to the powerful perception that our lives, health and ultimately our deaths are of us, about us, and are our own responsibility. Indeed, they articulate the very essence of our being – our individuality. This is not to say that in smoking or drinking alcohol people articulate a wish to die. Yet it is possible to say that such a model of life and death is reliant on a broad cultural sense of an individualized progression, a sense of time-frame or scale that is underwritten by the personalized sense of death. Thus, tobacco and alcohol advertisements, and images which satirize them, tend to draw on the same discourses with differing aims: in consumption practices that are figured as dangerous, people are positioned so as to experience themselves as individuals – finite beings who are nonetheless shaped by their own will, that is, their choices to smoke, to give up smoking, to drink alcohol or to abstain.

But the theme of risk and death, and forms of textual address that reference them, receive a positive discursive charge in other ways. What is key, I suggest, is the way in which the theme of death draws on a wider discursive currency that functions precisely to delimit the human (as mortal, with finite social circulation) from the thing or object (figured as non-mortal, with a potentially infinite social circulation). In effect, the theme of death restates and shores up what is perceived to be the dangerously unstable boundary between the categories of person and thing. My analysis here adds another dimension to Appadurai's (1986) framework of the circulation of things and Kopytoff's (1986: 66) 'cultural biography of things'. Studies such as that of Hallam and Hockey (2001) persuasively argue that the durable status of objects means that they are often used by individuals as material, enduring props in attempts to assuage anxiety at the impermanence of human life. In my analysis I am emphasizing how advertisements function as means of demarcating the boundaries of person and thing and in their referencing of risk or death in relation to some consumption practices, paradoxically reinforce a sense of individuality and vitality. The potentially infinite circulation of things functions as a contrasting and defining border for another category of circulating (finite) subjects – persons. Thus, rather than marking certain forms of consumption as dangerous, advertisements or health campaigns which mobilize death as a theme may conversely produce an appealing address that reassuringly rehearses the strict *distinctions* between those categories of person and thing. Walter Benjamin places death and the play of the organic against the inorganic at the centre of his analysis of fashion, the commodity-form and fetishism:

> Fashion prescribed the ritual by which the fetish Commodity wished to be worshipped. . . . It stands in opposition to the organic. It prostitutes the living body to the inorganic world. In relation to the living it represents the rights of the corpse. Fetishism, which succumbs to the sex-appeal of the inorganic, is its vital nerve; and the cult of the commodity recruits this to its service.
>
> (Benjamin 1973: 166)

For Benjamin, commodities are deeply implicated in the cycles of fashion, novelty and demand for the new. The sex appeal of the inorganic – the commodity – seduces the living body and tries to impose the rights of the corpse, that is, the will of the object in its animated commodity-form. I am suggesting that both the appeal and the threat of the inorganic, and the lure of advertisements which appear to represent them, lie in their capacity to adjudicate between the classifications of person and thing and to demarcate their boundaries. Here, death is that which provides the ultimate marker of the person and that category's distinction from that of thing or commodity. Ironically, the threat of addiction is figured as more ominous and more of an affront to the self-expressive individual in these discourses than the threat of death. The horizon of death is that which individuates and gives meaning to lives whilst addiction is cast in health campaigns and regulatory imperatives as the loss or atrophying of agency and individuality. Addiction is thus figured as effacing the opportunity – that we are all obliged to take – of living our own individuality through our free choices and our 'normal' death. This is less an issue of 'lifestyle' than a style of mortality, a style of living that is defined by our ultimate endpoint and the potential risks we may take in our consumption choices.

To reiterate, I am arguing that the widespread concerns about advertising's perceived powers, and the intensifying discourses about consumer pathologies such as 'shopaholism', are part of an elaborate rehearsal of and reflection upon the forms of relation between persons and objects, persons and images. The way in which advertising is conceived as breaching the correct or 'healthy' distance between persons and objects (or substances such as tobacco and alcohol) through persuasion provokes considerable cultural anxiety and drives for regulation. Mark Seltzer has argued (1992: 21) that academic and popular discourses operate, 'a principle of scarcity with respect to agency and personhood that the nature/culture division serves to protect'. Hence, the nature/culture antinomy frames the attribution of agency as a zero-sum game: objects are denied agency on the basis that, and to the precise extent to which, agency must be exclusively reserved for humans. This draws its force from the tension generated between the supposed polarities of nature and culture. But, Seltzer argues, it not the opposition between the terms that generates such cultural anxiety – what provokes this anxiety is precisely the fear, and indeed recognition, that they are not strictly distinct categories and are in fact inextricably implicated in one another's constitution. I am suggesting, then, that advertising draws so much criticism and regulation partially because it restates the anxiety-provoking recognition that, in contemporary understandings, the boundaries between the classes of objects and persons are permeable, and more troublingly, function as mutually constitutive. This vexing relation between persons and things, and consumers and commodities, is of course part of broader projects of defining the category of 'person' that have been occurring across multiple sites and in multiple registers. My focus here is the specificities of advertising's work of division in this dynamic: advertising mediates the anxiety about the erosion of a person's agency (particularly through encouraging 'compulsive' consumption or the consumption of 'addictive' commodities) and appears to animate objects and give them powers to act against the consumer.

Antidotes to advertising and the maladies of representation

This sense of advertising's power is paradoxically reinforced by the strategies of regulatory bodies such as the Advertising Standards Authority. By censoring advertisements, the regulatory drive implicitly gives recognition and legitimacy to a perception that advertising is a highly powerful force. In attributing power to those texts, regulations substantialize advertising and convince people more fully of advertising's influential and indeed manipulative role. In parallel, initiatives which aim to curb certain consumption practices draw on this belief in the power of images and use the same strategies and assumptions as advertising agencies. For instance, the establishment of the Health Education Council in Britain in 1968 was a response to a 1963 report that argued that advertising techniques should be deployed to promote health (Beattie 1991). More recently, the UK government's response to the Health Select Committee's Second Report on the Tobacco Industry and the Risks of Smoking (October 2000, command paper, Cm 4905) has been precisely to deploy the advertising industry's own representational tactics: 'we believe that the Department should examine the ways in which the agencies have marketed their advertising to this sector [tobacco consumers] and copy some of their most successful strategies'. This represents a considerable financial investment in health campaigns but also a strong institutional endorsement of the belief that advertising can directly influence behaviour. Advertising is thus deployed to counter the very effects of advertising. Many health campaigns are positioned as antidotes to advertising's 'misrepresentation' of consumption, or the way in which advertising is thought to obscure the 'truths' of consumption of certain commodities such as cigarettes. But such campaigns are not universally accepted as efficient ways of altering people's behaviour. Many of those who are responsible for creating such campaigns are very aware of the complex of social and economic factors influencing the consumption of 'dangerous' commodities, and subscribe to the view that an advertising campaign on its own will have a limited effect on altering behaviour (see Maibach and Parrott 1995). My concern here is not to provide a detailed assessment of health campaigns, nor to attempt to isolate their social effects. Instead, I am focusing on the circulation of understandings of advertising and the interests articulated in this circulation.

It is clear that since at least the 1970s, the British government has been aware of several reports which demonstrate that health advertising campaigns have very disappointing results (Beattie 1991). A report of a Health Education Council consultation exercise argued that such campaigns were ineffective and therefore unjustified and went on to critically explore the policy implications of these failures. There is even evidence that the British government attempted to suppress one 1973 report that came to the same conclusions (ibid.). Resources continue to be directed into health promotion campaigns despite awareness of their inadequacies and despite the findings of many studies of the crucial link between social structure and health that cannot be addressed through health campaigns. The former Director of the Health Education Council, David Player, argues that the British government consistently attempted to downplay the significance of social causes of ill-health, such as the link between unemployment and poor health, and even pressurized him to discontinue HEC press conferences which highlighted such causes (Pattison and Player 1990). Beattie (1991: 170) argues that the pursuit of discredited strategies 'regularly finds enthusiastic champions in Parliament', and continues for reasons of political expediency: such campaigns appear to be straightforward means of influencing behaviour that achieve high public profile. Indeed, Deborah Lupton (1995) suggests that health campaigns are designed primarily to function as public relations exercises whereby a government invests in high visibility strategies to convince the public that it is addressing key health issues such as drug taking or alcoholism: 'a glossy, attention-attracting television advertisement, bearing the logo of a department or health authority, is tangible evidence of action, even if it only denotes that money is being spent' (Tulloch and Lupton 1997: 33). For example, Dally (1995: 214) argues that anti-drug advertising campaigns are not primarily aimed at drug users – such campaigns are aimed at 'ordinary people' to reassure them that the government is acting on a serious problem. Corporate interests are also implicated in these high profile health campaigns. The tobacco company Philip Morris produced television advertisements which ran in the US in 2002 using the tag-line, 'Think. Don't Smoke'. At that time, The Philip Morris Company produced the second largest television advertising campaigns directed at discouraging children from smoking. But there is scepticism about the motivation of such campaigns: some media commentators have criticized Philip Morris' estimated $100 million a year expenditure on deterring underage smoking in the US as a public relations ploy.

Advertising is thus used as a site for the articulation of politically-charged issues such as the promotion of health – or social engineering – and public relations exercises. And despite controversy about health campaigns' lack of identifiable success in altering behaviour, advertising still remains a crucial site of intervention and of regulation. As I have argued, this is in part due to political expediency and advertising's appeal to governments as a relatively straightforward and high profile way of being seen to address social problems. But it is also based on an ingrained and generalized belief in the power of images. For example, several European cancer research groups have recently united to push for changes in health information on cigarette packets. They wish to follow the example set in Canada and Brazil where cigarette packets carry graphic images of lung tumours and diseased gums.[5] The presumption is that shocking images of the potential health impact of consuming cigarettes will deter smoking behaviour and counter the effect of cigarette advertising. This demonstrates a widely held and deeply rooted belief in the power of images to influence behaviour. Indeed, many official reports explicitly draw on this belief and institutionalize it as common knowledge. A report commissioned the UK Health Education Authority and written by an academic (Amos 1992), functions in precisely this way. Its remit was to explore the effects of images of smoking and advertisements of tobacco and alcohol in young people's magazines. Drawing on widely circulating beliefs about advertising and images more generally, it makes broad claims about their effects upon behaviour. The report takes as its starting point, and uses as its conclusion, the statement that, 'it is widely accepted that images of tobacco and smoking, from advertising, promotion and other sources, play an important role in determining rates of smoking among young people' (Amos 1992: 18). As I argued in Chapters 2 and 3, there is considerable disagreement about the possibility of isolating advertising's effects. I do not intend to rehearse these issues here as I am more concerned with highlighting the way in which images are perceived to exert a powerful influence and with analysing the potential effects of the circulation and institutionalization of this belief.

I have argued that one such effect is the framing of advertising as pathological, and a corollary of this is the framing of health campaigns as the antidote or cure for advertising. Here advertising is accused of multiple transgressions, most notably the way it is assumed to erode the safe distance between commodity and person by contaminating the flow of information between them. Advertising is thus figured in regulatory regimes, popular discourses, and many academic registers as obscuring the truths or realities of consumption and warping the lines of communication through which such information may pass. For example, the Director General of the World Health Organization has said that 'tobacco addiction is a communicated disease – communicated through advertising, promotion and sponsorship'.[6] In parallel, many health campaigns are discursively framed as attempts to combat such pathologies of communication and understanding. I would suggest, then, that the sense of a proliferation of pathological consumer practices, and advertising's perceived complicity in producing and maintaining this regime, operates on many levels including that of textuality and signification. In an analysis of AIDS discourses, Paula Treichler calls this emphasis on the textual an 'epidemic of signification' (cited in Haraway 1991: 203). This signals another key way in which the forms of relationality between 'person' and 'thing' are articulated – in many accounts, advertising is figured as an information system relaying between person and thing. Yet this information system corrupts the data about commodities. Goldman (1992: 202), for instance, argues that 'advertising dedicated to generating sign values is routinely grounded in a language disorder, the continuous rerouting of signifiers and signifieds'. This is a malady of signification in which advertising's textual sophistry is thought to distort the healthy flow of information and encourage addictive consuming practices such as smoking or drinking alcohol. Writing in the context of technoscience and focusing on immune systems, Donna Haraway (1991: 212) argues that 'disease is a sub-species of information malfunction or communications pathology; disease is a process of misrecognition or transgression of the boundaries of a strategic assemblage called self'. Translating this observation to the context of the pathologization of advertising and consuming practices, it provides a useful way of conceptualizing the perceived relationality between person and thing. Framed by regulators and by health campaigns as a communications disorder or pathology, advertising frames articulations of addiction as a disease of information. Addictive practices are thus thought to transgress the previously inviolate boundaries between self and substance (such as tobacco). Addiction is thought to invert the correct or healthy relationship between person and commodity: the person should rightfully consume and attribute meaning to the commodity whereas, in addictive consuming practices, the commodity is thought to reverse that flow of agency and information and act to define, use and consume the person. Hence tobacco or alcohol defines 'the addict' as a specific class of person and, in parallel, the flows of information and definition between person and thing are perceived to be contaminated and diseased. Channelling this corrupted information, advertising (and images more generally) come to be framed as the pathogen that diseases culture.

As noted above, health campaigns attempt to counter advertising's pathological effects with a dose of 'healthy' advertising in a kind of hair-of-the-dog logic. This is instanced in a series of images based on the theme of smoking cessation commissioned from twenty artists by the World Health Organization in 1999. The initiative called 'ArtWORKS' derives from the WHO European Partnership Project to Reduce Tobacco Dependence and is part of what the World Health Organization sees as a 'pioneering project which brings art, health, and culture together to tackle one of the major causes of death and disease in the world today'. The images produced are striking contributions, and indeed interventions, in the discursive circulation of understandings of tobacco consumption, bodily integrity, and representational impact. Albeit in more nuanced, more multi-layered ways, the images draw on the same conventions and discursive currencies as advertising images and the assumptions implicit in the regulations designed to restrict them. In one image by Russian artists Komar and Melamid (Figure 4.7), a famous Van Gogh self-portrait is reworked. We are exhorted to 'LOOK AT VAN GOGH AND DO NOT SMOKE', and at the foot of the image the text reads, 'the healing power of art™' underscored by the signature of the two artists. The World Health Organization banner at the foot of the frame of all the images reads, 'If you want to stop smoking ask how', making explicit the health promotion angle of the set of images. Known as an impassioned or even compulsive person prone to self-mutilation, Van Gogh is an unlikely role model for curative artistic intervention. But the force of the image does not reside in any specificity of Van Gogh as artist. Indeed, by using the trademark sign and their own signatures, Komar and Melamid aim to disrupt ideas of authorship and originality. Instead, the image is drawing on a generalized belief in the power of images – whether art or advertising – to impact for good or ill on individuals and society. The healing power of art, as they frame it, is deployed to combat the information maladies or communications pathologies which circulate through images and in particular through advertising. Here, art is the representational antidote that is used to cure those information disorders. But what is being targeted by the image's curative effects is not solely the distorted or incomplete information about consumption practices that advertising is thought to disseminate. It is not simply that tobacco advertising jams the communications lines or diseases the information flow and thus effaces what are seen as the truths of cigarette consumption – illness, addiction and death. The image references the communicative flows of agency that circulate between images (such as advertisements), objects or substances (such as tobacco) and persons (here framed as consumers). As noted above, such pathologies of communication can be seen as a

Figure 4.7 ArtWORKS World Health Organization anti-smoking campaign, 'Look at Van Gogh and do not smoke. The healing power of art' (courtesy of the artists, Komar and Melamid, and the World Health Organization)

'process of misrecognition or transgression of the boundaries of a strategic assemblage called self' (Haraway 1991: 212). This breaching of the (strongly defended, if provisional) boundaries of self, substance and image is the pathology of representation that art is imagined to cure. The representational impact of art is hoped to restore the healthy distance between self, substance and image by curing the malfunctioning flows of information that constitute those categories.

This dynamic is played out though many of the ArtWORKS images and is particularly evident in an image of a sculptural work by the artist Lisa Milroy (Figure 4.8). Here a cigarette packet, box of matches and a full ashtray created from clay and oil paint is underscored by a large text that reads 'STILL LIFE'. The image is reminiscent of the often cryptic form of address of cigarette advertisements, and indeed the image may intentionally cite and subvert that advertising strategy. Whilst referencing the still life of artistic convention, the line also references the life stilled by death – a death from smoking-related illness. Indeed, the textured, tangible presentation of the smoker's paraphernalia emphasizes the materiality and indeed plasticity of those objects as well as the material form of the image. The image figures those objects as if they were protean life forms; as if they had become animate in direct proportion to the implicitly stilled, now inanimate existence of the human actor. This flow of animation and agency between person and thing is precisely that which generates anxiety: in regulatory drives, it is those categories that must be kept strictly segregated. Violations of those borders – such as in tobacco or alcohol addiction – are thus defined in terms of pathology and diseased flows of communication between what should be distinct, bounded categories of person, substance or object, and image.

Figures 4.7 and 4.8 both draw on a widespread understanding that images *do things*: that images and advertisements act upon individuals or channel their behaviour. The idea behind all the ArtWORKS images is, quite literally, that art works. Hence the images attempt to shore up the distinction between reality and representation that has been exposed as less of a strict dichotomy than a constitutive dynamic. They attempt to reveal the truths of smoking that are defined as ill health, addiction and death, but also as a pathological intermingling between self and substance, person and object. Many of the ArtWORKS images derive their visual impact or discursive strike-power through referencing this tension in subtle ways. In a photographic piece by Wim Delvoye (Figure 4.9), a classic 1950s cartoon image of a boy smoking a cigarette is embroidered onto a piece of raw meat. The meanings generated by the image are multiple and overlapping. The brute materiality of the meat references the physicality, vulnerability and impermanence of the body, susceptible to consumption practices which may compromise its integrity as a correctly functioning unit. Yet the meaty materiality is not simply overlaid with the supposed immateriality of representation in the form of the boy image. The representation of the boy is also clearly tangible and indeed material for it is quite literally thread sewn into meat to form an image. This draws attention to the involution of representation and what is seen as the baseline truth or touchstone of what we are – material, flesh. Thus Delvoye's work makes explicit that which is implicit in the concerns about advertising images – the object–image, and

Figure 4.8 ArtWORKS World Health Organization anti-smoking campaign, 'Still life'
(courtesy of the artist, Lisa Milroy, and the World Health Organization)

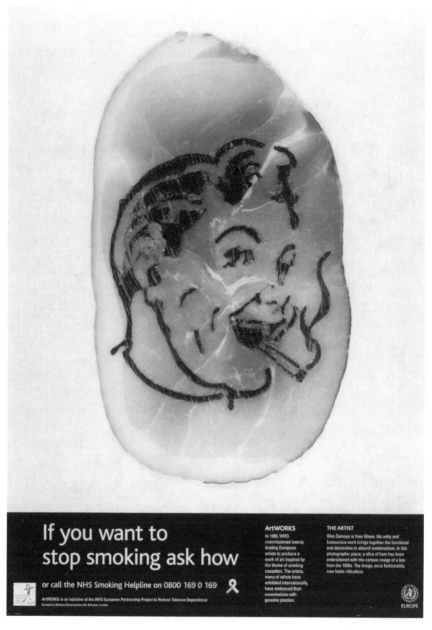

Figure 4.9 ArtWORKS World Health Organization anti-smoking campaign (smoking boy image) (courtesy of the artist, Wim Delvoye, and the World Health Organization)

subject–object polarities are more breachable and permeable than we care to recognize. But it also implies that the representational disorders or communication diseases in the flows of agency between person and thing are *in themselves* seen as pathologies: they do not require the referent of alcohol or tobacco addiction in order to be named as pathological or to generate concern. Ironically, therefore, the series of anti-smoking ArtWORKS images rehearses precisely the person–thing dynamic that causes controversy, but in doing so, displaces cigarette consumption from its perceived place as a key pathological practice, relocating it as just one pathology against a broad background of representational disorders.

This series of ArtWORKS images functions to highlight the work of art – the labour of representation – in constituting persons, objects and images and the forms of relationality between them. This work of constitution is what John Law and Ruth Benschop (1997: 175) call 'the representational labour of division'. In the following section, I explore how this representational work and these forms of relationality are framed though ownership and how part of the controversy around advertising derives from a sense that the relations between persons, images and objects, between life and death, can be *owned*.

Commodities, persons and ownership

The tension between objects, persons and images has long been recognized. Most famously, Marx wrote extensively about what he saw as the 'magic and necromancy that surrounds the products of labour' (Marx 1990: 169). For Marx, commodities were given form through the labour-power that was expended to create them: human labour coalesced into materiality, producing the form that we apprehend as a commodity.

> There is nothing left of them in each case but the same phantom-like objectivity; they are merely congealed quantities of homogeneous human labour. . . . All these things now tell us is that human labour power has been expended to produce them, human labour is accumulated in them. As crystals of this social substance, which is common to them all, they are values – commodity values.
> (Marx 1990: 128)

Marx understood the generation of both value and materiality to rely on this co-articulation. And neither were reliant upon the human actor to animate them in a unidirectional move. The value that human labour-power bestows on commodities is only activated in the human's *interaction* with material forms: 'human labour-power in its fluid state, or human labour, creates value, but it is not itself value. It becomes value in its coagulated state, in objective form' (Marx 1990: 143). In effect, human labour and materiality fuse in an alchemical way to produce a new amalgam or hybrid – the commodity-form suffused with value. It is crucial to understand the significance of Marx's view of labour-power, for as Spivak argues (1987: 154), 'labor-power is not work (labor), but rather the irreducible possibility that the subject is more than adequate – superadequate – to itself'. For Spivak, then, Marx's understanding of the subject centres on its capacity to produce more than itself, to be more than the sum of his/her parts, to have capacities that extend beyond the conventionally conceived boundaries of the subject. I think one way this could be usefully interpreted is through the person–thing tension that I have outlined throughout this chapter. The extended capacities of the human to which Marx seems to gesture can be conceived as the reaching out and intermingling of human and material form that fuse to create the commodity. Marx was clear that the material form of commodities should not be innocently conceived as a base, physical substratum, or brute materiality. The classification of 'the commodity' is not simply defined as an object that is produced in order to be sold. The form of commodities is a more complex fusion of human and object through the materialization of labour-power: 'the communal substance of all commodities, i.e. their substance not as material stuff, as physical character, but their communal substance as *commodities* and hence *exchange values*, is this, that they are *objectified* labour' (Marx 1978: 271–2, emphasis in original). The fusion of human labour-power and object creates a new compound – a commodity – which has become animated in that process of amalgamation. This newly activated form is not merely a prosthetic empowerment of the human, extending that human's capacity to act. The commodity may sever that relational commitment and may act upon its own volition and according to its own interests. In effect, the congealed labour-power of man takes on an independent existence and it 'begins to confront him as an autonomous power; that the life which he has bestowed on the object confronts him as hostile and alien' (Marx 1992: 324). In parallel, commodity fetishism obscures the ways in which commodities have been constituted. Marx was clear about the fusing of human labour into the material form of the commodity, and how the physical appearance of the commodity effaced that human value. In commodity fetishism, Marx argued, commodities themselves appear to generate their own value independently of human actors. Indeed, they come to function as actors in an exponential relation to the evacuation of human essence from subjects – that is, their objectification. In this same vein, Haug (1986: 42) argues that commodity fetishism animates the commodity, veils the human input in its production, and 'the illusion is maintained that it is the things as such which change by themselves'. Product innovation therefore appears fascinating and inevitable, and advertising practitioners play on this animation by attempting to attach personalities to brands (see Moeran 1996). Donna Haraway has taken up this analysis, highlighting the active forms of relationality between things and humans that are central to Marx's analysis:

> Commodity fetishism is a specific kind of reification of historical human integrations with each other and with an unquiet multitude of non-humans, which are called nature in Western conventions. In the circulation of commodities within capitalism, these interactions appear in the form of, and are mistaken for, things. Fetishism is about interesting 'mistakes' – really denials – where a fixed thing substitutes for the doings of power-differentiated lively beings on which and on whom, in my view, everything actually depends.
>
> (Haraway 1997: 135)

Haraway highlights how commodity fetishism does not merely conceal the human labour that has been invested in the production of commodities. More precisely, commodity fetishism obscures, and indeed denies, the involution of humans and non-humans that define that process of production.

In contemporary accounts, the brand has often been the focus of the concern about commodity fetishism. Brands and trademarks conceal the commodity's origins of production whilst attributing their ownership elsewhere. In effect, brands and trademarks stabilize value and meanings and function to fix legitimate authorship over that mark (Coombe 1998; Lury 1993). The development of trademark and copyright laws enable corporations (and governments) to protect the visible display of differentiated commodities and restrict access to words and images that come to be legally associated with them (Coombe 1998). I would argue that brands and trademarks serve an important function in the maintenance and organization of the boundaries between persons and things. They attempt to manage and channel the flows of information between persons and things in at least two key ways. By differentiating one product from another similar product, brands and trademarks produce a taxonomy of things. For instance, the advertisements in Figures 4.2 and 4.3 draw on and play with the brand name Silk Cut in an attempt to differentiate it from other makes of cigarette. But, as I have argued, the advertisements also function to produce distinctions between the categories of person and thing. In the contemporary proliferation of brands, and hence the proliferation of types of thing named *as thing*, the category of person is secured by the stating and restating of its differential status in relation to that of thing. The brand and trademark implicitly reference a human as their author and owner (either singly or collectively in the form of a company), and this relation of ownership further states the classificatory person–thing distinction.

As Haraway (1997) has elegantly and powerfully argued, branding is a key point of articulation of power, persons, and things, and can even organize access to, and understandings of, life processes in genetic research. Her concern is not with a general analysis of consumer culture – her research on technoscience aims to expose, amongst other things, the imbrication of gender, race and power in and through the brand. My concern rests more broadly with advertising and consumer culture and from this point of entry, I would suggest that branding needs to be seen as just one part of the multiple and at times contradictory processes at work in the circulation of value, materialities, persons and meaning. Indeed, branding functions as a temporary stabilization of this circulation. Hence, branding's role in consumer culture has often been given undue emphasis and there is evidence in some accounts of a kind of fetishism of the brand.[7] Approaches to consumer culture that privilege branding as their (sometimes exclusive) focus of analysis and point of critical intervention risk reproducing the very logics they aim to criticize. By focusing on the brand and the advertising text as privileged analytic site, some academic accounts reify advertising as a cultural form, abstracting it from its complex commercial context, and flattening it out into a logic of equivalences or a reductive analytic currency. As a form of fetishism, such an approach empties out the concept of branding and then attaches to it particular analytic values. This ascribes enormous critical purchase to the analysis of advertising texts: advertising and branding come to be considered symptomatic of 'Culture' and readings of brands (in isolation from any other commercial or symbolic processes) are thought to offer a privileged insight into that culture.

Branding, therefore, must be viewed as only one element in a complex of commercially circulating elements. For some, branding represents the ultimate form of fetishism in which economies have become 'de-materialized' or rely more heavily on symbolic resources such as brands than on material resources such as factories. Slater (2002) criticizes such approaches for their emphasis on the ownership of cultural and symbolic capital – in the form of brands – rather factories and other material resources. Even companies such as Nike and McDonalds that invest considerably in the symbolism of their brand names also co-ordinate massive apparatuses of production and distribution. Seen in this light, we cannot view such economies simply as 'de-materialized', that is, reliant primarily on signification and symbolic values such as brands (Slater 2003). Thus brand fetishism, I argue, obscures the *relationality* of multiple factors that act to constitute both a commodity and an advertisement: processes of research and design; production and distribution; consumers' acts of purchase, use and display; acts of disposal; advertising practitioners' promotional rhetoric; practitioners' hesitant and contingent beliefs in and about advertising; regulatory actions; general perceptions about the power of advertising. These and many more factors combine to (provisionally) stabilize the commodity-form as object and the advertisement as image. In the spirit of Latour's (1993) notion of translation, it is perhaps appropriate to suggest an adaptation of Haraway's (1997: 142) understanding of a gene to help apprehend the form of a commodity and of an advertisement as, 'a node of durable action where many actors, human and non-human, meet'. It is also important to recognize the historical depth of this articulation. Elsewhere, I have referred to this relationality of objects, human agency, feelings and images as a form of alchemy: historically embedded materialities, social institutions and structures of feeling mingle and fuse to form new hybrid commodities which nonetheless carry those interwoven histories of privilege and subordination with them (Cronin 2002a). A commodity and an advertisement are therefore best considered as a nexus of historically embedded but evolving forms of relationality between multiple elements.

In these dynamic relationships, neither commodities nor advertisements should simplistically be considered actors, but it is nevertheless important to recognize their active status in dividing up the world into persons, objects and images. Hence, the critical attention that brands and advertising draw is not only based on their perceived status as images in a powerful visual culture or on their powers of de-materializing capital. To reiterate, branding and advertising draw their discursive force and critical impact from their articulation of the forms of relationality between persons and objects, images and materialities. More precisely, they enact and prominently display *ownership* of the relationships between those persons and objects, images and materialities. Marilyn Strathern (1999: 140) employs the concept of 'property relations' to think through the processes of contextualization and decontextualization involved in the flow of knowledge about products:

Ownership re-embeds ideas and products in an organism (whether a corporation, culture or individual author). Ownership gathers things momentarily to a point by locating them in the owner, halting endless dissemination, effecting an identity. We might even say that emergent forms of property signify new possibilities for corporeality or bodily integration in lives that observers constantly tell themselves are dispersed.

(Strathern 1999: 177, emphasis in original)

For Strathern, contemporary commercial property relations produce an intensified connection or relation between persons and things. I would argue that this connection is the management of the form of relationality between things and persons through ownership: by asserting that only persons (and not things) have the capacity to own, the concept of ownership does the work of restating the strict classificatory boundaries between persons and objects. Hence, academic criticism of brands and branding implicitly derives its force from the unsupportable perception that the relation between persons and objects is articulated in commercial terms and is structured by profit and ownership. Conversely, what many consumers of branded products may find appealing about them, alongside their much-discussed functions of display of status and group belonging, is exactly their promise of ownership of the forms of relationality between persons and things, images and materialities.

Therefore, when individuals are ascribed the status of compulsive or addictive consumers (thus pathologizing the act of possession), or are drawn into the supposed pathological relations produced by advertising images, a broader concern about ownership is being articulated. This is a concern about the ownership of the relationships between persons, things and images, and is articulated on multiple levels: corporate, individual, national, environmental. This feeds into the widespread concern about the power of (advertising) images which translates into a perceived crisis of *ownership* of the forms of relationality between persons and objects, reality and representation. For example, control of the relationship or distance between reality and 'mere representation' is crucial in terms of corporate liability. Tobacco firms being sued by individuals who have suffered disease from smoking base their claims in part on the fall from reality that advertising is thought to engender. This is often framed as a distancing from the real by a concealment of information and by manipulative persuasion. It is estimated that tobacco companies in the USA have already been forced to settle $130 billion of claims from state governments to pay for health costs of treating smokers, a claim which is in part based on the perceived effects of tobacco advertising (*The Times*, 14 June 2002). As I have argued, such advertising is thought to warp the correct or healthy flow of information between consumer and commodity. Indeed, images are imagined to wield such enormous power that those involved in advertising practice are also considered susceptible to its effects in surprising ways. For instance, the model who became the face of R.J. Reynolds Winston brand cigarettes in the USA between 1978 and 1980 attempted to sue the company for $65 million damages. He claimed that he has been overwhelmed with feelings of guilt and responsibility for the deaths of people who were persuaded to smoke by his youthful, healthy image (Goodwin 2002). This extraordinary example of litigious culture raises fundamental issues around the belief in the power of images and advertising in particular. It would be interesting to speculate as to the proportionate invulnerability of tobacco companies to litigation had they never advertised their product. This notion of liability is increasingly articulated in terms of risk which is framed as a scientific means by which to assess exposure to danger (Douglas 1992).[8] Framing individuals' practices in terms of risk assessment and management places emphasis on the availability of accurate information on which to base this assessment. Hence, advertisements – already widely understood as mendacious and manipulative – are placed under an intensified pressure to offer information or an accurate presentation of the 'truths' of consumption.

Throughout this chapter, I have argued that pathology and risk are located by regulators and critics in forms of relationality – in the *way* in which elements of commercial circulation are seen to connect. In this flow, the person–thing dynamic is one key site through which concerns about advertising are articulated. Advertising is imagined to erode the boundaries between person and thing and to corrupt the traffic of information that flows between them and which constitutes those very distinctions. Those boundaries are tacitly recognized as contingent and fragile: 'what counts as a "unit", a one, is highly problematic, not a permanent given. Individuality is a strategic defence problem' (Haraway 1991: 212). Thus, the mutable nature of what is cast as a singular unit – a person or a thing, for example – causes considerable concern and elicits defensive tactics such as those exhibited in initiatives like advertising regulation. The drive for regulation forms part of a long-standing concern about images in general, channelling perceptions of retrograde social developments. Foreshadowing contemporary discourses circulating in regulation, Debord (1994 [1967]) argues that the images which make up the spectacle collapse the proper distance between self and the outer world (a world of commodities). Spectacle erases the boundaries and distinctions crucial to human existence:

> The spectacle erases the dividing line between self and world, in that the self, under siege by the presence/absence of the world, is eventually overwhelmed; it likewise erases the dividing line between true and false, repressing all directly lived truth beneath the real presence of the falsehood maintained by the organization of appearances.
>
> (Debord 1994: 153)

Debord's analysis is a forerunner to more recent accounts that follow the logic that 'the spectacle is the *chief product* of present-day society' (Debord 1994: 16, emphasis in original). In such accounts, signs rather than materialities are the essence of capitalist production and consumption. I have argued that such analyses insufficiently examine the relations between images and materialities, advertisements and commodities, and too hastily assume the ascendance of images and signs in proportion to the decreasing significance of materialities. This development is part of long-established tensions in the forms of relationality between things, persons and images.

Appadurai (1986) argues that by focusing on the transformation of the consumer through various promises (such as increased sex appeal or enhanced sense of belonging), advertising fetishizes the consumer rather than the commodity. However, I have argued that the most forceful impact of advertising lies in its staging of the *relations* between consumer and commodity, person and thing. Thus it is neither the commodity nor the consumer that should take the primary place in an analysis of consumer society, but rather the contingent, mutable forms of their relationality. It is in this sense, I suggest, that the social life of commodities is intimately intertwined with the constitution of human social life and with the constitution of the category of person. Whilst we are used to considering how advertising and consumption mediate understandings of group and individual identities such as that of class distinction, less attention has been directed at their articulation of the broader social distinctions between 'person' and 'thing'. Baudrillard (1988: 45, 46, emphasis in original) argues that, in consumption, 'need is not need for a particular object as much as it is a "need" for difference (the *desire for social meaning*)' and thus 'consumption is a system which assures the regulation of signs'. For Baudrillard, this is an over-arching representational scheme or a play of difference in the domain of signification. I have argued that such a production of difference – particularly the distinctions between the classifications of person and thing – should not be seen as Baudrillard's meta-discursive, relatively stable framework, but rather as a historically and culturally specific, protean delineation of the category of 'person' in relation to that of 'thing'. Discourses of compulsion and addiction instance a specific articulation of this relationship. Moreover, this delineation does not operate through strict oppositions, but rather through nuanced and heavily freighted understandings of the imbrication between categories. In the realm of consumption, then, the category of person is constituted with recourse to understandings of the commodity as not precisely a mark of the inviolate boundary between thing and person; rather this constitution is enacted through a tacit, underlying recognition of the commodity's vexing status as ambiguously animated. Commodities trouble the relations between the animate and the inanimate, the alive and the not-quite-alive. In Marx's terms, commodities have been invested with human labour and become quasi-animate forms which may come to act with an independent will against their creators. This could be seen as a 'politics of synthetics' in which synthetics represents at once a man-made fabric and the fabrication of 'man' as type or classification in the play between categories. As I suggested in Chapter 1, this is an emphasis on the *making* of distinctions – not just on an abstract relationality – which acquires a particular impact or currency under capitalist systems of exchange.

In reassessing the distribution of animation and agency between the categories of person, thing and image, I do not want to suggest that agency should be unproblematically attributed to things and images. Indeed, the troubling of ideas of human agency in the work of influential thinkers such as Judith Butler (1993) has had an interesting impact upon contemporary analyses. It is possible to read this as an analytic moment in which the agency of the subject has become so problematized that a shift of critical attention to the potential agency of *objects* could be seen as somewhat appealing. But an approach that figures the object as straightforwardly agentic is unproductive: it artificially arrests the flow of animation, agency, and power for analytic purposes. Agency would then become *property* of objects and understandings of the complex forms of relationality and flows of information between persons, things and images would be foreclosed. Instead of considering these issues through the rather static, rigid concept of property, I have explored them through the more mutable framework of ownership. I have argued that the controversies over, and also the appeal of, consumption and advertising images partly derive from their emphatic foregrounding of the *ownership* of the relations between persons, objects and images. Ownership offers an imagined control of the vexing involution of the classifications of persons and things. This has been played out in many sites but has taken its most potent form in slavery where particular understandings of the categories of person and thing have been articulated and reproduced through ownership and exchange (see Kopytoff 1986; Sheller 2000). In parallel, advertisements appear to animate things, thus engendering anxiety but also fascination and delight. As I have emphasized, the relationships between the classifications of person, thing and image constitute only one element of the dynamics of consumer culture. However, those relationships play a key role in organizing the social field and an analysis of their articulation may offer some understanding of why and how social distinctions continue to be played out and reproduced through consumption. It is to this issue that the final chapter turns.

5 Advertising reconsidered

Throughout this book I have argued that the circulation of beliefs in advertising actively constitutes advertising as a social and economic institution and co-ordinates its manifestation in textual forms. I have not attempted to construct a general theory of advertising, but instead have focused on three key elements: controversy, regulation, and the vexed relations between the categories of 'person' and 'thing'. Departing from Barthes' (1974) classic use of the concept of 'myth' to denaturalize the ideologies of advertising texts, I have explored how advertising myths – the complex circulations of belief and commercial imperatives – organize, and materially form, the advertising industry and its regulation. Thus, the 'myths' of advertising are not falsehoods or misrepresentations in any straightforward sense: they function as mobile power–knowledge formations that allow for the rehearsal of understandings of social relations (including advertising's own influence in the social realm) and produce classificatory structures. I have not, therefore, taken a direct approach to the heavily freighted question of 'does advertising work?' Such a framing of the analysis would risk fetishizing and endorsing the very techniques of measuring advertising's effects that engender so much debate and controversy in the industry itself. Instead, I have asked the question, 'what is the work of advertising?' This reframing of the analysis opens up new questions about the social impact of advertising, and demonstrates how the very uncertainties about advertising's commercial effects actively constitute the form of the industry and the advertisements it produces. I have shown how such insubstantial and amorphous phenomena as beliefs and understandings impact materially upon the commercial success and social acceptance of advertising. In Chapter 3, I argued that practitioners' views of advertising operate on multiple levels that are not reliant on fixed benchmarks of veracity or feasibility. Their understandings of advertisements' form and function are formulated and circulated as what I have called 'promotional beliefs' and 'invested understandings'. As Michael Schudson (1993) has argued, advertising operates as a form of capitalist realism in which advertising does not so much represent society *as it is* but society as it *should be* according to capitalist principles. Advertising does not function, then, by reproducing reality, but by presenting ideals and offering images of 'life and lives worth emulating' (Schudson 1993: 215). If Schudson's analysis is correct – and I think that it is – arguments that advertising misrepresents society, for example by reproducing social stereotypes, are misplaced. By extension of this argument, advertising cannot be said to stimulate consumption by encouraging people to *believe* in the product. Similarly, people do not need to believe that advertising will present them with the necessary information about a product or service. People do not even need to believe in the values that are presented to them. Indeed, disbelief of advertising's claims and values will not short-circuit capitalist cycles of production and consumption, hence Adorno and Horkheimer's (1997: 167) indignant remark that people feel compelled to buy products 'even though they see through them'. The implication in Adorno and Horkheimer's account is that compulsion or persuasion function not through illusion or misrepresentation but despite it – the management of consumers' beliefs is not a necessary part of capitalist stimulation of consumption.

In my analysis, I have adapted Schudson's (1993) account of capitalist realism to explore, first, practitioners' invested beliefs about advertising and how these are integrated into their practice, and second, how claims about advertising circulate between clients, agencies and the public. In the second element, agencies' promotional rhetoric about the efficacy of their research and creative production operates in the sense of a Foucaultian truth claim. In this dimension, agencies attempt to persuade potential clients collectively of the efficacy of advertising as a means of promotion. Simultaneously, agencies generate promotional rhetoric about the truths they claim they can deliver about the target market in order to compete with other agencies for those clients' business. In the first element, practitioners' personal beliefs in and about advertising function less as truth claims than as invested understandings. These are personal investments in their understandings of the social value of their job and their sense of social responsibility, as well as material investments that translate into financial rewards and occupational mobility. There is no imperative for practitioners to *believe in* the power of advertising because these invested understandings are not founded on any sense of advertising 'as it is' – any sense of an inalienable essence or commercial baseline truth – but rather on ideals of advertising form, practice and effects. As a type of capitalist realism, these understandings are based on advertising as it *should be* and not on any claim to reality as it is. But whilst it is not necessary for practitioners to be personally convinced of the veracity of advertising's claims or promises, or of the efficacy of advertising in increasing sales, their beliefs in and about advertising should not be seen as 'false'. Instead, they are what I have called 'promotional beliefs'. Here, I base my definition of promotion on Andrew Wernick's (1991: 182): promotion is 'a complex of significations which at once represents (moves in place of), advocates (moves on behalf of), and anticipates (moves ahead of) the circulating entity or entities to which it refers'. Adapting this definition, I have argued that practitioners' promotional beliefs *represent* and *advocate* advertising in that they are deployed as currency in the promotional matrices that circulate between clients and agencies and within agencies between Creatives, Planners and Account Managers. These promotional beliefs are intimately involuted with advertising practice and materially produce advertising as cultural and economic form. These beliefs *anticipate* advertising in that they present ideals or future-oriented perspectives of the world that advertising imagines or aims to create. This is an ideal capitalist world of consumption and choice, in which practitioners can predict and deliver consumers' wants that are, in turn, always articulated through commodities and commercial services. These promotional beliefs, then, promote advertising as a means of social resolution, and a means of stimulating the economy, of offering informed choice to consumers, and of providing entertainment and pleasure. Practitioners are themselves deeply invested in these understandings whilst simultaneously promoting them to clients, to consumers and to a sceptical public. These understandings are not 'false' or duplicitous in any straightforward sense for they do not encompass any claims to truth: they project forward to new, ideal worlds in which the logics of commercial promotion, production and consumption are married in harmony.

In this context, I have suggested that the motivations behind, as well as the practices involved in advertising need to be understood as a part of a circuit of belief. As I argued in Chapter 2, regulatory bodies such as the Advertising Standards Authority draw on popular beliefs about advertising and public standards of taste and decency as benchmarks for acceptable advertising. These beliefs are deployed to support the ASA's self-regulatory regime and to deflect initiatives that push for statutory rather than self-regulatory structures. In turn, drives for stricter advertising regulation in the UK have marshalled the political will and public support for statutory regulation – such as the Tobacco Advertising and Promotion Act (UK Government 2001) – by drawing on general perceptions that advertising directly influences the consumption of products. These beliefs are also evidenced in the newly agreed Framework Convention on Tobacco Control that imposes global restrictions on tobacco advertising. There is evidence of a general contemporary belief that advertising is a powerful social and economic force but, as I demonstrated in Chapter 1, the perception that advertising is a potent force in either stimulating consumption or altering social mores is relatively recent. Nineteenth-century Euro-American societies considered consumer motivation or the causes of compulsion to be multiply located in the new sites of consumption such as the department stores; in the lure of the material form of the commodity itself; and in the weaknesses or pathologies of individuals. But in contrast to contemporary understandings, such accounts very rarely figured advertising as an important motivating or compelling force. These nineteenth-century beliefs had material effects as they conditioned regulatory responses to consumer culture and projects of social control.

In parallel, academic analyses are implicated in these circuits of belief in at least two key ways. First, moves to regulate advertising deploy academic studies as supporting evidence of advertising's pernicious social effects. I have highlighted one significant study that cites advertising agencies' internal documents as statements of fact (instancing advertising's considerable power) and as evidence of intent to manipulate consumers (see Hastings and MacFadyen 2000a, 2000b). This approach achieves only a partial analysis as it ignores the parallel function of such documentation as promotional rhetoric designed to enhance agencies' profile and attract clients. The circuit of belief about advertising comes back upon itself when agencies themselves cite government regulatory imperatives as evidence of advertising's persuasive power – as one Senior Creative in my study put it, 'when it's right, it's powerful. It must be, or else they wouldn't be trying to ban [tobacco] advertising'. Second, just as practitioners 'believe' in advertising, so also academics 'believe' in the power of theory or academic analysis to lay open to scrutiny the complex institutions and commercial and creative practices involved in advertising. In a sense, these are also promotional beliefs and invested understandings as their authors set into competitive circulation their own analyses. Like the advertising industry, academia functions – amongst other things – as a self-promotional arena in which publications and renown translate into higher salary, higher status and greater occupational mobility. At the end of this chapter I return to this issue and consider the implications for analyses of advertising.

In Chapter 4, I explored 'the work of advertising' as an enabling device for popular, regulatory (and academic) debate about contemporary society and social divisions. There I argued that advertising campaigns for 'dangerous commodities' such as tobacco and alcohol draw their discursive force from understandings of the conceptual distinctions between persons and things. This dynamic is particularly evident in the advertisements' referential relation to the concepts of compulsion or addiction. Thus part of the work of advertising is based on marking boundaries between the categories of person and thing, consumer and commodity. Advertising works to deny the interrelationship of the concepts and obscure the complex implication of each in the other's constitution. Thus the person–thing dynamic also functions as a myth: it is not a falsehood, but rather a mode of signification in which understandings of what it is to be a 'person' and a 'thing' are constantly stated and rearticulated. The circulation of these myths 'substantialize' those categories and, on a more immediate and sensuous level, co-ordinate the framework within which the classification 'person' is experienced by human agents. Seen in this context, it is possible to appreciate how the themes of danger, death and risk employed in anti-smoking campaigns (and some tobacco advertisements) may have an unintended impact. Instead of deterring smokers by shock tactics, such images may restate a reassuring categorical distinction between persons and things by signalling the finite, mortal status of persons that contrasts with the potentially infinite social circulation of things. The theme of death thus reiterates and supports a sense of humanity in what is often perceived (negatively) as an increasingly *material* world of things. The regulatory targeting of advertisements for 'dangerous commodities' can be seen, then, as a health initiative but also as means of demarcating the category of 'person' from that of 'thing'. This human subject is characterized by free will that, in turn, risks being compromised by 'addictive' commodities. Furthermore, this conceptual category of 'person' is challenged by objectification – the imagined encroachment of the category of 'thing'.

I have argued that by appearing to animate commodities, advertising disrupts the established distinctions and social hierarchies of type and classification. In this context, regulatory drives such as those of the Advertising Standards Authority frame advertising as an insidious cultural and economic form that engenders maladies of textuality, or figure it as a form of diseased communication that fosters social pathology. In this regime of regulation, the communication disorders thought to be cultivated by advertising are addressed by a dose of good or 'healthy' images such as health education campaigns. These wholesome campaigns are not merely thought to replace or challenge the dangerously corrosive effects of advertising, but are understood to actively *cure* them. But the paradoxes of regulation are all too clear. In analysing the twentieth-century battle against 'repression' in the realm of sexuality, Foucault (1990a: 159) has argued that 'the irony in this deployment is in having us believe that our "liberation" is in the balance'. Regulatory imperatives for controlling advertisements for 'addictive commodities' such as tobacco function in this way, setting free will or agency in opposition to the effects of consuming tobacco or alcohol, and offering liberation through increased censorship. The paradox of the regulatory focus on the power of advertising images and its perceived textual sophistry in promoting 'dangerous consumption' is that it allows the proliferation and *disaggregation* of those substances or practices that are understood to be addictive or pathological and allows the concept of addiction to circulate more fluidly. In citing advertisements as prime motivators of addictive or compulsive consuming practices, the full force of regulatory control falls on those textual forms. Thus in shifting the imagined site of addiction from the substance itself (alcohol, tobacco, the commodity) to its advertising – to the level of textuality – the regulatory strictures paradoxically enable new forms of circulation of those discourses. By identifying the advertisement (the textual artefact itself) as the source of the industry's social and commercial impact, the regulations intensify understandings of advertising as a dangerous representational form that corrodes the distinctions between the classifications of 'person' and 'thing' and fosters unhealthy or 'addictive' relations between consumers and commodities. By casting tobacco (and alcohol) advertising as dangerous, and by drawing attention to its disruption of type and taxonomy, regulations amplify a sense that *all* advertising threatens the classificatory orders of the social. Ironically, this expanded scope of cultural anxieties and associated regulation forces advertising and marketing to further proliferate new promotional practices and thus engenders intensified concern about the allied taxonomic breakdown. Therefore, by focusing exclusively on advertising images and text, the regulatory bodies in fact precipitate the *broadening* of the scope of compulsion and understandings of 'addictive' consumption. In the following sections I expand upon the arguments made in preceding chapters and consider the implications for creating more nuanced understandings of advertising.

Cultures of addiction? Consumption, representation and crisis rhetoric

As noted in Chapter 1, Foucault's (1990c: 144) analysis of the birth of 'the dangerous individual' charted a series of shifts 'from the crime to the criminal; from the act as it was actually committed to the danger potentially inherent in the individual; from the modulated punishment of the guilty party to the absolute protection of others'. This development expanded the regulatory scope from rare and monstrous figures to encompass more common everyday figures such as 'the degenerate' or 'the pervert'. 'The addict' is now part of that register of dangerous individuals, representing a threat to social order and cohesion and focusing considerable social disapprobation. But unlike some nineteenth-century under-standings of kleptomaniacs explored in Chapter 1, the most significant distinction in this framework is not that between legally responsible subjects and legally irresponsible subjects. Rather, it is between 'absolutely and definitively dangerous subjects and those who can cease to be dangerous provided that they receive certain treatment' (Foucault 1990c: 144). The figure of the addict thus mandates regimes of treatment in order to neutralize his or her threat to society. It is possible to see this as the expansion of disciplinary surveillance over individuals as part of projects of social control. For instance, the figure of the female addict has consistently been considered a threat to 'modernity, capitalist production, social reproduction, and democratic citizenship', an anxiety focused through the perception that drug use impedes or contaminates women's social role as mothers (Campbell 2000: 14). But as Keane (2002) argues, the perceptions of 'what's wrong' with addiction vary according to the type of addiction, the social positioning of the subject of addiction, and the type of discourse. These concerns about addictive consumption practices become distilled and surface sporadically as specific social panics (Jenkins 1999). These discursive skirmishes in projects of social control have material effects as Fraser and Gordon (1997) demonstrate in their analysis of 'dependency' discourses. US social policy, they argue, figures 'welfare dependency as post-industrial pathology' (1997: 136) by drawing on discourses of drugs and addiction. Dependency on welfare thus becomes inflated into a 'behavioural syndrome' which is both avoidable and blameworthy and from which claimants should be weaned (ibid.: 139). This discourse of dependency now has a considerable hold on the popular imagination and thus offers a powerful currency for political rhetoric – as the then Vice President, Dan Quayle, commented on the 1992 Los Angeles' riots: 'our inner cities are filled with children having children . . . with people who are dependent on drugs and on the narcotic of welfare' (cited in Fraser and Gordon 1997: 138–9).

From a different analytic position, Jacques Derrida explores the conceptual nexus of addiction and reality, arguing that what we hold against the drug addict is,

> . . . that he cuts himself off from the world, in exile from reality, far from objective reality and the real life of the city and the community; that he escapes into a world of simulation and fiction. . . . We do not object to the drug user's pleasure per se, but we cannot abide the fact that his is a pleasure taken in an experience without truth.
>
> (Derrida 1993: 7–8)

Analyses such as that of Fraser and Gordon's (1997) clearly point to projects of social control in which groups are managed through the ascription of identities such as 'addict' or 'welfare dependent' and their subsequent subjection to state control. Derrida here examines how the social animosity and regulation levelled at the addict derives from his or her perceived withdrawal from reality into illusion and consequent disconnection from the social bond. Living 'in illusion' and expe-riencing the 'false' pleasures promised by drugs challenges conventional sociality and becomes subjected to forms of social control and public censure. But the concept of addiction has broken free of its exclusive referents of alcohol and drug consumption and has expanded into the everyday, mainstream world of 'normal' citizens who had previously been protected from 'dangerous individuals' such as addicts. In a popular register, we are constantly told that we risk becoming addicted to everyday substances such as sugar or chocolate, and ordinary practices such as exercise, sex, watching television, or shopping. A headline in the British newspaper the *Observer*, states that 'one woman in five is a shopaholic' and that 'the percentage of the population suffering from the serious medical condition of shopping addiction is reaching crisis point, overtaking the number of drug and drink addicts in the UK combined' (McVeigh 2000). Another newspaper article states that, 'it used to be drink and drugs. But these days it seems we're hooked on sex, work and food . . . have we become addicted to addiction?' (Kenny 2001).

The notion of addiction or compulsion is also mined for consumer appeal by producers and advertising agencies and thus becomes further disseminated in the popular register. Perfumes appear to represent a particular nexus for these tropes: Armani has launched a perfume called 'Mania' whilst Dior has launched another called 'Addict'. Gucci's perfume 'Rush' draws not only on associations of drugs and (glamorous) addiction, but on the experience of (drug) consumption – the rush (see Figure 5.1). The trope of addiction also has resonance in other commercial contexts. In a promotional catalogue for women's sportswear called 'The Encyclopedia of Addictions', Nike playfully references all manner of consuming

Figure 5.1 Gucci perfume advertisement, 'Rush' (courtesy of Gucci)

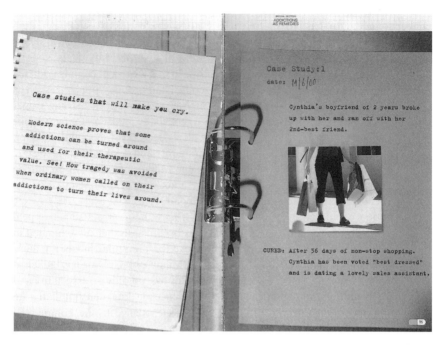

Figure 5.2 Nike 'Encyclopedia of Addictions' image, 'Case studies that will make you cry' (courtesy of Nike)

addictions. Masquerading as a rather dull academic journal with a plain cover, the catalogue reveals its identity at the foot of the cover with a small 'swoosh' Nike insignia and text that reads, 'Not Actual Publishers'. In a section called 'addictions as remedies' (Figure 5.2), we are presented with a case study which reads:

> Case studies that will make you cry. Modern science proves that some addictions can be turned around and used for their therapeutic value. See! How tragedy was avoided when ordinary women called on their addictions to turn their lives around. Cynthia's boyfriend of 2 years broke up with her and ran off with her 2nd-best friend. CURED: After 36 days of non-stop shopping. Cynthia has been voted 'best dressed' and is dating a lovely sales assistant.

Nike here takes 'expert discourses' on addiction and addiction therapy and turns them around in a playful way. The catalogue acknowledges women's consuming pleasures and the tensions in popular understandings of the delineation of 'normal' consumption as opposed to excessive, pathological or addictive consumption. In another section of the catalogue entitled 'diagnosis', a trope of pleasure is aligned the classic ideal of moderation or balance in consumption (Figure 5.3). The text reads, 'I am addicted to things that are good for me. I am addicted to things that are bad for me. Therefore my life is in balance.' The popular and medical axiom of

Figure 5.3 Nike 'Encyclopedia of Addictions' image, 'I am addicted to things that are good for me. I am addicted to things that are bad for me' (courtesy of Nike)

moderation in consumption is here referenced and reworked by Nike. Like Figure 5.1, the Nike images do not cast the addict as a marginal figure or 'dangerous individual' – the criminalized, exceptional status of the addict is replaced by a notion that we are *all* addicts of one sort of another (whilst retaining the risky, dangerous associations of addictive consumption that is the source of its appeal to marketing and advertising). Paradoxically, the regulatory controls on advertising enable the disaggregation and dissemination of notions of danger and addiction in the same manner as these (uncensored) images. Indeed, the proliferation of discourses of addiction in the popular register is mirrored by the expansion of expert knowledges designed to cure them. Alongside increasing numbers of therapy groups, there is a growing number of popular self-help books for compulsions such as gambling addiction, sex addiction, and co-dependency as well as shopping compulsions boasting such striking titles as *Women Who Shop Too Much: Overcoming the Urge to Splurge* (Wesson 1990).

Clearly, this contemporary expansion of notions of compulsion and addiction does not constitute a major historical break in the trajectory of addiction-attribution. As I argued in Chapter 1, the perceived causes of compulsion in the nineteenth century shifted fluidly between site, substance and individual debility or pathology, and encompassed 'ordinary' practices such as shopping and its potential degeneration into oniomania (shopping mania). But the contemporary proliferation of so-called addictive substances and practices points to some interesting articulations of consumer culture. Why should the rapid expansion of addiction discourses appear at this historical point? Some analyses suggest that 'the drug' constitutes a meta-category of discourse, inextricably bound up with the issue of representation itself. For Derrida, the question of drugs is perhaps *the* question, the question of writing. The *pharmakon* – understood as drug (both medicine and poison) and as writing – has no essence of its own for 'the *pharmakon* is the movement, the locus, and the play: (the production of) difference' (Derrida 1981: 127). Thus in Derrida's analysis, the category of 'drug' is that which structures the structure of the possible and the very possibility of representation itself. In this paradigm, 'the drug' is a blank conceptual space encompassing both the positive (cure), and the negative (pathology, addiction). Here the drug has no essential form and hence, 'no one has so much as defined drugs, and this is in part because they are non-theorizable' (Ronell 1992: 59). On another level, Eve K. Sedgwick (1994: 135) suggests that we may begin to address the question of 'why now?' by looking at 'the peculiarly resonant relations that seem to obtain between the problematics of addiction and those of the consumer phase of international capitalism'. Sedgwick is here speculating that addiction may be reliant upon capitalism's systems of international (legal and illegal) trade in order to supply the raw materials necessary for the continued compulsive relationship to a substance.

A politics of synthetics

This book has not attempted a detailed exploration of these well-established debates about drugs and addiction but rather has focused on certain key interconnections between advertising, consumption and notions of compulsion in order to closely examine the role of advertising in the social. I have taken as my focus the conceptual tensions between persons, things and images, arguing that these tensions animate contemporary dynamics of consumption, pleasure, anxiety and regulation. Many accounts of advertising obliquely address these issues by hinging their analyses on loss, fall, or contamination: use-value is eroded and increasingly replaced by exchange-value; the significance of production is displaced by consumption; a sense of our own natural or organic human needs is lost to artificially created desires; material forms become less significant proportionate to the growth in importance of images, signs and brands. In Judith Williamson's (2000: 70) influential analysis, advertisements play on our vulnerability and innate psychic lack or loss by objectifying us and offering us back an ideal, unified image of ourselves: 'since parts of you have been claimed as separate by advertisements, in order to get back these "lost objects" you must buy them and recreate yourself out of your own "spare parts"'. In Williamson's psychoanalytic account, the way in which lack or loss is inscribed at the heart of subjectivity chimes well with the general perception that advertising parasitically erodes the essence of the self. But the popular and academic perception of loss in relation to consumption and advertising, I suggest, is not founded on a psychic essence of subjectivity, but derives (at least in part) from socially and historically specific understandings of the categorical distinctions between 'person' and 'thing'. Leiss *et al.* (1990: 5) touch on this in their claim that advertising is 'the discourse through and about objects, which bonds together images of persons, products and well-being'. But I have argued that advertising does not function solely by associatively conjoining persons and commodities to create images of well-being or identity. Advertising also operates as a mechanism for demarcating the categories of 'person' and 'thing', 'consumer' and 'commodity' in alignment with capitalist ideals of purchase, ownership and use. In Chapter 4, I explored this person–thing dynamic by analysing how contemporary understandings of images and personhood frame perceptions that advertising animates commodities. I argued that advertising is thought to breach or corrupt the healthy distance between persons and things, and between persons and representation. I read this as an unbearable affront to the ideal of the self-contained individual whereby things and substances are perceived to impinge on the self. Anxieties about advertising images and the regulation that these anxieties elicit are thus part of a rehearsal of the relations between persons, things and images in which the ideal of the unitary, firmly bounded category of person is continually demarcated and defended. Advertising is cast by regulations as a representational disorder and social pathogen that erodes or contaminates the healthy or correct relation between persons and things. The irony in this formulation is that advertisements themselves come to be seen as pathological without any necessary reference to 'addictive' or 'dangerous' commodities such as alcohol or tobacco. Advertising in general thus comes to be increasingly framed as 'dangerous', as a form of pathogen that erodes social structure, taxonomic order, and the integrity of the unitary individual.

In the context my analysis, Derrida's argument that society's disapprobation of the addict is founded in their perceived flight from reality and existence in fantasy can be seen in another way. I have argued that the controversies over consuming compulsions in nineteenth-century discourses partially derived from their signalling of the potential democratization of privileges of illusion, consumption and pleasure. The figure of the addict represents an unsettling merging of person and substance, consumer and commodity, casting the life of the addict as one spent in a state of illusion detached from reality. However, this capacity for unsettling relations and drawing censure is not reserved exclusively for those deemed addicts, but extends the status of 'dangerous individual' to the ordinary consumer thought to be in thrall to the deceptions of the commodity. But this state of illusion is not merely bound to the 'false' or artificial pleasures that have so often been associated with consumer society. As I have argued in Chapter 1, this exclusive state of illusionism refers also to a mode in which we may apprehend the intimate relations that exist between persons and things: in a mode of illusion that animates commodities and objectifies persons, we may recognize our kinship with things that has been constituted by long-established understandings of unitary personhood whilst being simultaneously denied by them. As Latour (1993: 11) argues, this is a continual process of 'purification' which demarcates humans from non-humans and marks them as distinct, impermeable categories or types. Arbiters of social reality insist on the absolute inviolability of these categories, but this very insistence is productive of that which is abhorred: 'the more we forbid ourselves to conceive of hybrids, the more possible their interbreeding becomes' (Latour 1993: 12). Whilst Latour's is a general analysis of the constitution of human and non-human distinctions, my account focuses on the distillation of many of these categorical tensions into the commodity-form with the emergence of consumer capitalism. Existing in a state of illusion thus refers, amongst other things, to a capacity to see hybrids, to recognize the human labour that constitutes the human–thing amalgam that is the commodity, and to see through the gloss and appeal of commodity fetishism. This is not to suggest that addicts and consumers who feel compelled by 'animated' commodities have a privileged access to understanding the truth of the social. Rather, it is to propose that conceiving of social relations must include not only the bio-politics of social control at the level of 'life' or the species-being, but also the person–thing relations that constitute our conception of the social. As I suggested in Chapters 1 and 4, these relations can be seen as a 'politics of synthetics' in which synthetics represents both a man-made fabric, and the fabrication of 'man' as classification and type, that occurs in the play of that categorical dynamic. This politics of synthetics is a means of controlling both singularized bodies and populations in the manner of bio-politics, but also offers control over the conceptual benchmarks of type, genre and classification that order the social realm.

In this context, advertising functions by drawing on our invested understandings of who we are. This appeal to our sense of self operates on the level of individualized identity synchronous with that of the species-being, and takes as one key point of articulation the construction and protection of the conceptual distinctions between persons and things. As I argued in Chapter 1, this distinction is not an essential, transhistorical characteristic of human personhood, but takes on a particular form and resonance in consumer capitalism. One powerful articulation of the person–thing relation instanced in advertising is the imagined collapse in notions of compulsion and addiction of the strict boundaries between 'person' and 'thing'. All advertising has come to be perceived as dangerous in this way but, in relation to 'dangerous commodities' such as tobacco and alcohol, the negative impact is distilled and amplified. Subject and substance are perceived to merge; the standard logic in which the consumer acts upon the commodity is reversed, and the distinctions between human agent and thing – a dynamic relation that is constitutive of what it is to be human – are eroded. David Lenson has suggestively argued that the term 'addiction' can be etymologically traced to the Latin verb *addicere* (to say or pronounce, to decree or bind), indicating that 'the user has lost active control of language and thus of consciousness itself, that she or he is already "spoken for", bound and decreed. Instead of *saying*, one *is said*. The addict is changed from a subject to an object' (Lenson 1995: 35, emphasis in original). Setting aside reservations about the scope and analytic purchase of etymological approaches, Lenson's comments usefully highlight a key element of my analysis of advertising and commodity relations.[1] Part of the popular and academic concern about what is seen as increasing commodification, I suggest, articulates an anxiety about objectification in a broad sense. The imagined atrophying of the subject and its reduction to the status of an object expresses concerns about a perceived encroachment of things into boundaries of the category 'person'. The popular critique of expanding commodification cannot then be understood merely as a collective disinclination for exponentially increased purchase of commodities: buying commodities and services seems to be well established as a social norm and has become a positive and indeed pleasurable experience for many (see Falk and Campbell 1997; Miller 1998, 2001). Instead, perceptions of a loss of territory in the imagined zero-sum game of agency-attribution are key to understanding the generalized critique of 'expanding commodification'. In this tense dynamic between persons and things, commodity culture is seen to represent a loss of humanity directly proportionate to the gain of the material world: humans are diminished, their essence apparently leeched out of them by strangely animated commodities, as the material world of things augments its hold over us. In this discursive tug-of-war, advertising is cast as a prime culprit, drawing fierce criticisms and demands for regulation. But just as the human subject is thought to be diminished by the disintegration of its agency and consequent relegation to object-status, restorative attempts for that subject are set in motion. Writing about the growth of addiction-attribution, Sedgwick (1994: 133) calls this reactive move the 'propaganda of free will', in which propaganda is to be understood in the precise sense of 'the imperative that the concept of free will be propagated'. In the context of my own argument, this also refers to the propagation of the species-being who, defined by free will and active subjectivity, is challenged by the perceived threat of hybridization with things. This is a politics of synthetics – an inter-species form of bio-politics – in which the world of things is imagined to menace the integrity of the population of humankind.

Advertising thus speaks to a broad understanding of the condition of humanity and social relations. Raymond Williams (1980) has argued that advertising – the magical system – is representative of a general failure of society to attend to human needs, aspirations and sociality:

> If the meanings and values generally operative in . . . society give no answers to, no means of negotiating, problems of death, loneliness, frustration, the need for identity and respect, then the magical system must come, mixing its charms and expedients with reality in easily available forms, and binding the weakness to the condition which has created it. Advertising is then no longer merely a way of selling goods, it is a true part of the culture of a confused society.
>
> (Williams 1980: 190–1)

For Williams, advertising exists to bolster and ratify capitalist social relations, representing the rotten core of capitalism and its inexorable erosion of humanity. This is connected, I argued in Chapter 4, to a parallel root of popular concern that resides in the fear that individuals or corporations are increasingly becoming enabled to *own* the terms of the relationship between persons and things. Thus criticisms of advertising and branding, I suggest, articulate a deeply rooted popular antipathy to the institutionalized power over persons and things that capitalist modes of production and promotion represent. Therefore, part of the popular criticism of advertising can be seen as a correct but *displaced* understanding that people are the (literal) raw materials of capitalism. Advertising cannot be said to literally animate things and dehumanize people, although this is the generally circulating perception. But advertising represents and advocates capitalist forms of production and exchange that operate their alchemy in precisely this way. Indeed, it was the apprehension of capitalist societies' reduction of persons to raw materials or base matter that motivated some of Marx's most trenchant criticisms. Capitalism, he argued, 'knows the worker only as a working animal – a beast reduced to the strictest bodily needs' (Marx 1970: 73). To extract the optimum degree of profit, workers' pay was calculated precisely at, and not above, the level necessary for survival and hence reduced definitions of their needs to 'the barest and most miserable level of physical subsistence' (Marx 1970: 149). Humans come to be treated as things just as their labour-power is extracted to produce the things – commodities – which enable the flow of capital. As I have noted, recognizing this dynamic of animation and objectification is often cast as a form of 'illusion' when consumers orient their worlds around material goods and their hybrid relations with persons. Indeed, seeing the forms of connection evident in commodity fetishism – seeing through the illusion that commodities are 'born' without the human input of the labour of production – is censored by capitalist society.

Throughout this book, I have argued that advertising as institution and textual form is constituted by the circulation of 'advertising myths' understood in Barthes' (1974) sense of myth. For Barthes (1974: 143), myth does not represent falsehoods but rather operates as a signifying device: 'myth does not deny things, on the contrary, its function is to talk about them'. In my analysis, therefore, myths are the currency through which understandings of social relations, and advertising's role in those relations, circulate. They are the points of tension through which understandings of the vexed relations between the categories of 'person' and 'thing', consumer and commodity, are rehearsed and adapted. These myths include regulatory rhetoric about advertising's effects, practitioner's promotional and self-promotional accounts and practices, and popular and academic criticisms of advertising's effect on the social fabric. Hence, these advertising myths are neither false nor artificial, but are active agents that reconstitute social forms and structures through capitalist ideals and principles. In this system of ratification, advertising becomes a key index of the normal, the benchmark of the taken-for-granted, of the everyday, of the inevitable. It is such an established part of ordinary life in the West that just by dint of being advertised, products and services are brought into everyday systems of understanding and are thus normalized. Advertising may achieve this feat not through any textual sophistication, but merely by touching the product with its associations of everydayness, of acceptability. Products may be subject to criticism (and high-profile advertising may simultaneously expose products to increased censure), but they are also offered protection by the naturalizing, normalizing function of advertising. Hence, whilst specific advertising campaigns for tobacco or alcohol products cannot be said to unambiguously increase sales of those products, their advertising does function to normalize tobacco and alcohol products and make them a part of the accepted cultural lexicon. Such advertisements act as a buffer against attempts to ban tobacco itself as they help to normalize it in the popular understanding, and thus help to counter any political will to ban the 'dangerous commodities' themselves. Conversely, advertising can act as a negative principle, conferring a dubious status on any commodities that do not submit themselves to its normalizing effect. Thus, the work of advertising is not confined to increasing sales of a product or service. Advertising provides other more diffuse commercial functions for producers including the conferral of symbolic legitimacy on a product.

Advertising and taxonomy

I have also argued that, alongside advertising's role as the index of the normal, advertising is simultaneously framed as dangerous, as a pathogen that atrophies or contaminates the social realm. Its perceived disruption of taxonomy is highlighted as a key way in which advertising threatens social order. The emphasis on person–thing distinctions that is so powerful in advertising foregrounds issues of type, specification and genre. As I argued in Chapter 1, nineteenth-century controversies around consumption and associated social change represented, amongst other things, anxieties about shifting taxonomies and boundary infringements: gender identities and roles were altering, class structure was decomposing and reforming into new hierarchies, commodities were thought to be acting upon consumers and encroaching onto the terrain of humanity. Controversies about consuming women thus had a dual focus that distilled concerns about the erosion of upper- and middle-class women's restriction to the domestic sphere and, as women were long-established guardians of taxonomic order, articulated anxieties about shifting modes of classification or stratification. Highlighting this emphasis on gender as type or classification, but also including other categories such as class, sexuality or nationality, reframes certain questions about power–knowledge: gender can be seen to function not only as an ascribed identity and social role that is subject to control, but also as one form of what Foucault has called 'matrices of transformations' (1990a: 99). According to Foucault, 'relations of power–knowledge are not static forms of distribution' and therefore 'we must seek . . . the pattern of modifications which the relationships of force imply by the very nature of their process' (ibid.). Gender is clearly a powerful means of sub-dividing the category 'person', but can also be seen as a classifying device with a broader impact. As nodes or meeting points of power–knowledge, it is possible to understand gender as an animating force, as type or classification that both transforms social structure and social relations, and is transformed by them. In a parallel, if not symmetrical way, race discourses manifested in slavery drew on and rearticulated definitions of 'person' and 'commodity' for the purposes of commercial gain and imperial expansion (see Kopytoff 1986). Seen in this way, power is not a property of, nor permanently possessed by, any social institution or group, but rather holds a transformative relation to evolving social formations and social identities. Gender operates as one important classifying device or matrix, and disquiet about women's shifting social position in the nineteenth century derives in part from an anxiety about the shifting of taxonomies that order the social.

As noted in Chapter 1, Franklin *et al.* argue that gender can function as 'a *productive mechanism* or *enabling device*' (2000: 7, emphasis in original). This is an emphasis on gender as type, genre, or classification. Here, my use of Foucault's notion of 'matrices of transformations' to consider one of gender's functions supplements this account by stressing not only gender's productivity or its enabling role, but also its capacity to foster change or more radical transformation. Elsewhere I argued that advertising is an important social form that organizes (gendered) access to the ownership of the status of 'self-possessive individual' (Cronin 2000a). Here I am emphasizing how advertising articulates and transforms relations between the material world and the category of 'person' within the framework of capitalism, engendering considerable controversy in the process. In this stress on gender, it is women who constitute the marked category. On a material level, women supply a high proportion of the world's (often unrecognized and unpaid) labour and thus literally form capitalism's raw materials. But I am also suggesting that the category of 'woman' – alongside other categories such as race and sexuality – is symbolically freighted with the task of classifying and ordering the social realm. This is most evident in nineteenth-century Euro-American societies where debates over gender were not merely mediated through the theme of consumption; those debates actively organized the material development of consumer societies.

This understanding of gender as both classificatory device and matrix of transformation is not intended to decentre the material concerns or the lived experience of women, nor to analytically displace the interests of class and power that suffuse contemporary society and are often articulated and reproduced through consumption. I believe that this approach *recentres* issues of gender, class, race and other socially significant classifications by drawing attention to the centrality of those categories in ordering the social world: those classifications are constituted by, and in turn constitute, the social realm and function to co-ordinate access to economic, social and symbolic resources. Distance to and from the privileged category of 'person' is strictly organized according to ascribed status of gender, class, sexuality and race (see Skeggs 1997). Important work such as that of Bourdieu (2000) shows how such classifications and their relation to social power and resources are played out through consumption. Social distinction is thus produced and reproduced through consumption patterns – material goods form the key site for this social dynamic as capitalism stores value in commodities and organizes access to value through the circulation of those commodities. But commodities also form such an important site of contest because they articulate the tensions in the conceptual relations between the categories of 'person' and 'thing'. These tensions are of course framed within capitalist structures, a fact most evident in the practices of slavery and the definitions of slaves as 'non-persons' – things to be bought and sold for profit. Therefore, the relations between commodities and their consumers are productive not just of social distinctions such as class; they are productive of the very category of 'person' (in tension with that of 'thing').

In parallel to social classifications such as gender, advertising itself can be seen as a matrix of transformation. Schudson (1993) argues that advertising functions as a form of 'capitalist realism' representing not society *as it is*, but society *as it should be* according to capitalist ideals. I have argued that advertising's role is more radical and more transformative than this. Departing from Schudson's account, I propose that advertisements do not merely present an ideal of capitalist society: advertising as institution functions by actively attempting to construct new social taxonomies and new modes of instituting those classificatory regimes. Moreover, I have argued that advertising itself functions as a transformative matrix that orders the person–thing dynamic and conditions the ways in which these interconnections constitute social relations. I have elsewhere called the commodity a site of alchemy or transformation, emphasizing the way in which the commodity-form both coalesces and transforms elements of production, historical privilege and subordination (Cronin 2002a). Here, I am placing emphasis on advertising's transformative role with regards to social taxonomy.

Following this logic, advertisements are not best understood as attempts to *represent* women (or to misrepresent women in social stereotypes). Instead, images of women in advertising operate, amongst other things, as transformative matrices in which social relations are made and remade, hierarchies constituted and reconstituted. The dual deployment of gender and of advertising as transformative matrices or ordering devices is aptly illustrated in a 'spoof advertisement' produced by the UK newspaper the *Observer* in a special feature on drugs called 'Drugs Uncovered'. To illustrate a possible future society in which today's illegal drugs have been transformed into common (legal) commodities, the newspaper created advertisements for drugs such as cocaine and ecstasy and positioned them as normal advertisements within the page layout. One such advertisement was for a 'Cokane' brand of cocaine (Figure 5.4). The spoof advertisement has all the familiar characteristics of advertising: a brand name ('Cokane', which plays on advertising and branding's common use of non-standard spelling in the style of the supermarket 'Kwik Save', for example); a striking image (of a female, semi-naked angel figure); a prominent tagline ('how pure are you?'); a promise of guaranteed quality ('100% pure Columbian cocaine'); associative and contrasting elements (the impurity of the fallen angel versus the purity of the product); and even a government health warning in the style of tobacco advertisements ('Government health warning. Cocaine can cause both short-term and long-term damage to your health. Short-term effects include increased body temperature and irregular heartbeat. Long-term effects may include liver damage. It is illegal to supply cocaine to anyone under the age of 18').

The Cokane advertisement illustrates advertising's function of ordering in multiple ways. Advertising's most familiar role is that of distinguishing and ordering types of commodity (for example, food/medicine) and distinguishing different brands of similar products. The advertisement for branded cocaine is included in this everyday classificatory process, rendering cocaine the equivalent of any other mainstream good in a striking or perhaps shocking way. As a form of capitalist realism, we are familiar with advertising's presentation of (capitalist) ideals such as abundant consumption, but this image makes explicit advertising's function not only of presenting ideals but of actively reconstituting boundaries of type and classification, of the legal and the illegal, of the normal/acceptable and the abnormal/unacceptable. But the force of the advertisement's impact also lies in its ordering of the classifications of 'person' and 'thing' or 'substance'. This is most

Figure 5.4 Cokane spoof advertisement, 'How pure are you? Cokane. 100% pure Columbian cocaine' (courtesy of the *Guardian*)

striking is its reference to drugs – a category of good generally perceived to be dangerous, having the effects of objectifying, dehumanizing, effacing the boundary between person and thing, and subtracting human essence from the individual. But the *Cokane* advertisement also foregrounds the prevalent sense that *all* advertising challenges and erodes those boundaries. In deploying a figure of a woman-angel hybrid, the image also signals gender's role of articulating type or specification: here, the non-human angel figure is hybridized with the category of human by referencing the female. This deployment foregrounds the way in which gender can function as what Foucault (1990a) has called a matrix of transformation. As such a matrix, gender as type forms the currency which allows the shifting play of signification between drug, commodity, danger, and bodily integrity, and actively reframes classifications of person and non-person.

But whilst person–thing relations represent a threat to the ideal unitary self, they simultaneously appear to offer positive dynamics. One of the great popular appeals of advertising and also of consuming commodities, I suggest, lies in their apparent promise of a discursive management of the unsettling relations between persons and things, the shifting dynamic between animation and objectification, and the mutable classifications of personhood and commodity-status. The illusionism involved in seeing the relations between persons and things offers ways of *seeing through* commodity fetishism, recognizing the labour embodied in commodities as Marx did, and thus acknowledging their person–thing hybridity. But this is not to suggest that, as in Marx's analysis, human fulfilment resides solely in our access to unalienated labour. Consumption, and its potential of managing relations between persons and non-persons, may also offer ways of realizing the species-being.

As I argued in Chapter 4, tobacco advertisements generate appeal by tendering not lifestyles precisely, but our own, individual styles of mortality. Through explicitly referencing bodily risk and mortality (exclusive characteristics of persons), these advertisements restate and shore up the perturbing and tenuous discursive boundaries between person and thing – they revalidate a notion of unitary personhood. But such articulations of the person–thing distinction do not require tobacco, alcohol or addiction as their referents in order to achieve discursive purchase. It is not just advertisements for 'dangerous' or addictive commodities that offer this form of typological resolution because advertising in general operates through this dynamic. As I argued in my analysis of the Cokane spoof advertisement (Figure 5.4), whilst shifts in type and classification may be received as unsettling and challenging to established discursive currencies, taxonomic changes are also read as opportunities for reforming the social according to new ideals. Just as advertising is perceived as a threat due to its apparent animation of commodities, so also does it appear to offer – by allowing the play of the person–thing dynamic – the promise of a new, enhanced human subject reconstituted through that which threatens it. Through its fraught encounter with the animated commodity, and also the threat of addiction or compulsion, the subject is decomposed and recomposed into a new strong amalgam in which the hybrid nature of this new person–thing amalgam is, of course, denied and censored.[2]

To be clear, I am not suggesting that differences between persons and things can be discounted, but rather that western thinking has instituted this categorical division that has subsequently been continually rehearsed and strongly defended. This issue of distinction confronts academic analyses in many forms. Marshall Sahlins (1976: 205) formulates the issue which, he argues, has long haunted anthropology (and indeed many disciplines) as a question of

> how to account for the functional relations between aspects that had at first been conceived as distinct. Much of anthropology can be considered as a sustained effort at synthesizing an original segmentation of its object, an analytic distinction of cultural domains it had made without due reflection.

The distinct, impermeable classifications of 'thing' and 'person' that have become firmly enmeshed in western societies risk embroiling academic studies in analytic tautologies and unproductive accounts of advertising and consumer society. I have attempted to account for how advertising manages and manipulates those long-established conceptual distinctions and substantializes them, or attempts to formulate them as *facts*. But as Foucault argues, 'man' as classification or type cannot be seen as an ahistorical essence for it will eventually disintegrate and be reformulated: 'man is only a recent invention, a figure not yet two centuries old, a new wrinkle in our knowledge, and . . . he will disappear again as soon as that knowledge has discovered a new form' (Foucault 2000b: xxii). This may appear a disheartening or disempowering position to take, but when accused of being a pessimist, Foucault responded by arguing that,

> My optimism would consist . . . in saying that so many things can be changed, fragile as they are, bound up more with circumstances than necessities, more arbitrary than self-evident, more a matter of complex, but temporary, historical circumstances than with inevitable . . . constraints . . . to say that we are much more recent than we think isn't a way of taking the whole weight of history on our shoulders. It's rather to place at the disposal of the work that we can do on ourselves the greatest possible share of what is presented to us as inaccessible.
>
> (Foucault 1990d: 156)

The contingencies and fragility inherent in the constitution of the category of 'man' thus open it up as a space of contestation. This highlights the politics of intellectual access to the processes by which the categories of 'person' and 'thing' are constituted and reconstituted. Haraway (1991, 1997) has mapped out the battles over commercial *ownership* of the relationship between persons and things and other feminist work has actively challenged the ex-centric and subordinate positioning of the category of 'women' in relation to that of 'person' and its associated privileges and rights (see, for example, Diprose 1994; Pateman 1988). Such struggles over conceptual benchmarks generates new questions about the relationships between materialities and persons.

In this book I have taken as a focus advertising's circulation of myths and particularly the contested relations between the classifications of 'person' and 'thing'. But my account also offers important insights for a more general analysis of advertising. I have argued that advertising has been framed as an easy target that channels multiple concerns and political issues. Advertising offers itself as an accessible and ubiquitous focus for concerns about ownership of the relations between persons and things. Whilst contemporary capitalism's web of institutions (for example, the World Bank), and flows of finance, information and people are far too complex for most people (including academics) to grasp, advertising presents itself as a highly visible cipher for these formations. In this context, the critique and regulation of advertising may offer a reassuring (if tenuous) sense that we have some control over capitalism's processes and development. In approaching such a complex of concerns and interests, I have argued for the importance of analysing the *circulation* of the various elements that constitute advertising as a social institution, textual artefact, and cipher or metaphor. This involves assessing how the elements *interact* – for instance, exploring how practitioners' promotional rhetoric impacts upon regulatory practices – not merely producing a discreet analysis of each element. This avoids reifying any one element as the essence of advertising and avoids artificially halting the flow of beliefs, capital and images that constitute it. Such an approach also offers a reflexive account of academia's own implication in the circuit of beliefs about advertising that in turn impact upon the practices in the industry and regulatory practices from both within and outside the industry. Analyses of advertising are often deployed by academics as theoretical shorthand for contemporary society (variously exemplifying the power of capitalism to manipulate, the dominance of visual culture, the influence of television, the scope of popular culture, the erosion of traditional social bonds). More radically, advertising as trope is used in academia as a classificatory device to typify the social and to demarcate social fields and areas of study: academic knowledges/commercial understandings, cultural issues/economic issues. By stressing the *circulation* of these understandings, my analysis points to the complexity of such imbrications and offers caution to less nuanced and more totalizing accounts of advertising as text and industry. Tracking the flow of myths, I hope that this book has tendered some insights into the antinomies of advertising and into the investments we have in analysing them.

Notes

Introduction

1 There have been some important ethnographic accounts of advertising agencies (Miller 1997; Moeran 1996; Schudson 1993; Tunstall 1964). See Chapter 3.
2 The Framework Convention on Tobacco Control was adopted by the 192 members of the World Health Organization on 21 May 2003. It requires countries to impose restrictions on tobacco advertising, sponsorship and promotion. Parties are required to move towards a comprehensive ban within five years in all but those countries whose constitution makes this unfeasible (for example, constitutions that defend free speech for commercial purposes). Such countries will be required to restrict tobacco advertising and promotion.

1 Images, commodities and compulsions: consumption controversies of the nineteenth century

1 I use the pronoun 'he' advisedly: in Benjamin's account, the figure of the *flâneur* is unambiguously male, embodying the male privilege of access to public spaces (see Wolff 1995).
2 The development of advertising cannot be understood, therefore, as the index of capitalism's inexorable rise: nineteenth-century advertising cannot straightforwardly be read as the (unsophisticated, underdeveloped) precursor of contemporary advertising in a kind of capitalist teleology (see McFall 2000).

2 Advertising as site of contestation: criticisms, controversy and regulation

1 This version of the Codes is the tenth edition which came into force on 1 October 1999, with amendments added on 23 April 2000. All further details about the ASA's remit and citations of its Codes refer to this document. New versions of the Codes are published regularly but consistently retain their general scope and content. I am here restricting my analysis to the Codes amended in 2000 as they framed and channelled the controversies around tobacco and alcohol advertising in the period leading to a ban on tobacco advertising in 2003.
2 All further citations of the ITC Codes and details of the Codes' enforcement refer to this document.
3 Unfortunately, these documents are now not available to researchers who may wish to analyse them.
4 In Chapter 3, I analyse the textual address of these Silk Cut advertisements and the complex, indeterminate relation advertisements have to consumption practices.

5 These concerns were made apparent in interviews I carried out with advertising practitioners, trade associations and regulatory bodies. I discuss this in detail in Chapter 3.
6 For example, see *Marketing Week*, 24 October 2002.

3 Advertising agencies: commercial reproduction and the management of belief

1 Marketing and advertising practitioners routinely fix upon new, supposedly infallible
methods for tracking the success of campaigns. Such techniques – a current favourite is
econometrics – are presented to clients as expensive but efficient means of proving that
advertising *works*, thus promoting the skill of individual agencies and the worth of the
industry as a whole (see Lury and Warde 1997; Schudson 1993).

4 Animating images: advertisements, texts, commodities

1 My analysis does not aim to explain why people continue to smoke (and drink alcohol)
despite an awareness of the severe health consequences, but it does offer an account of
the background against which such choices make sense.
2 This notion of the relationship between non-human actors and human actors has previously
been investigated in relation to consumption by Leiss in his account of a 'conserver
society' as an alternative to a consumption society (Leiss 1978: 112). In the context of mass
production and consumption and the ecological problems this engenders, Leiss argues for
a need to build 'a syncretic framework in which human needs are conceived in relation to
the needs of non-human nature' (ibid.).
3 Some analyses, however, suggest that the social life of humans does not terminate at death.
Hallam *et al.* (1999) argue that the social identities of individuals continue to circulate
through the practices and memories of the living.
4 Adbusters' website: <http://adbusters.org>
5 BBC news:
<http://www.bbc.co.uk/hi/english/health/newsid–2027000/2027680.stm> Accessed 14
June 2002.
6 <http://www.who.int/inf-pr-2001/en/pr2001-47.html> Accessed 18 January 2002.
7 There are notable exceptions to my generalized claim of ad or brand fetishism. For
example, Franklin *et al.* (2000) provide highly persuasive and nuanced accounts of
the work of the brand. I discuss these accounts and their implication more fully in
Chapter 5.
8 Risk has been widely debated in recent social theory, most notably by Ulrich Beck (1992)
who has analysed the relationship between the production and distribution of wealth and
the production and distribution of risk. It is not my aim here to engage in these wide-
ranging debates but rather to focus on the specificity of issues of danger and risk in the
circulation of advertising knowledges and practices.

5 Advertising reconsidered

1 Etymological approaches can offer fresh ways of looking at familiar terms that may open
up interesting avenues of analysis. However, that etymology offers a privileged analytic
point of access to the socially-embedded nature of a concept or associated practices is
less clear.
2 Furthermore, the much-discussed power of advertising to effect social control may be
more complex and perhaps more contradictory than it seems. Deleuze (1995) has argued
that contemporary Euro-American societies operate less as *disciplinary* societies in
Foucault's sense, and now more as *control* societies in which such control is effected
through communication. As I argued in Chapter 4, advertising is usually framed in popular,
political and regulatory rhetoric as a powerfully controlling force that operates through

(pernicious, deceptive) communication. But in many regulatory practices it is also seen as a pathogen of communication or a force disruptive to the correct flow of channels of information. Regulation and health campaigns are thus seen as 'antidotes' to advertising, or means of curing and redirecting the communications channels that advertising has corrupted. In effect, advertising is thought to be a controlling force in society but may, paradoxically, also short-circuit those very communication control devices.

Bibliography

Abelson, Elaine S. (1989) *When Ladies Go A-Thieving: Middle Class Shoplifters in the Victorian Department Store*, Oxford: Oxford University Press.

Adorno, Theodor W. (1991) *The Culture Industry: Selected Essays on Mass Culture*, edited and with an introduction by J. M. Bernstein, London: Routledge.

Adorno, Theodor W. and Horkheimer, Max (1997 [1944]) *Dialectic of Enlightenment*, trans. John Cumming, London: Verso.

Advertising Association (1994) *Ads and Fags: The Many Cases Against Banning Tobacco Advertising*, London: Advertising Association.

—— (1999a) *Position of the Advertising Association on Tobacco Advertising*. Online. Available HTTP: <http://www.adassoc.org.uk/position/tobacco.html> (accessed 25 August 2001).

—— (1999b) *Position of the Advertising Association: The Draft Council Recommendation 'Drinking Alcohol by Children and Adolescents'*. Online. Available HTTP: <http://www.adassoc.org.uk/position/alcohol2.html> (accessed 25 August 2001).

—— (2002) *Who We Are*. Online. Available HTTP: <http://www.adassoc.org.uk/whoare.html> (accessed 18 January 2002).

Advertising Standards Authority (2000a) *The British Codes of Advertising and Sales Promotion*. Online. Available HTTP: <http://www.asa.org.uk/the_codes/downloads/Bcasp_10.pdf> (accessed 10 August 2001).

—— (2000b) *Annual Report 2000*. Online. Available HTTP: <http://www.asa.org.uk/news/show_news.asp?news_id=70&news_section=all> (accessed 10 August 2001).

—— (2000c) *Adjudications*. Online. Available HTTP: <http://www.asa.org.uk/Adjudications/sh...d=all&from_index=by_sector&sector_id=2> (accessed 11 March 2002).

—— (2000d) *Adjudications*. Online. Available HTTP: <http://www.asa.org.uk/Adjudications/sh...d=all&from_index=by_sector&sector_id=2> (accessed 11 March 2002).

—— (2000e) *Self-Regulation: Advertising Under Control*. Online. Available HTTP: <http://www.asa.org.uk/self_regulation/self_regulation/index.asp> (accessed 10 August 2001).

—— (2000f) *Adjudications*. Online. Available HTTP: <http://www.asa.org.uk/Adjudications/show...id=all&from_index=by_sector&sector_id=55> (accessed 10 August 2001).

—— (2001a) *Annual Report*. Online. Available HTTP: <http://www.asa.org.uk/annual_report/ar_2001/complaints.asp> (accessed 12 December 2002).

—— (2001b) *Adjudications*. Online. Available HTTP: <http://www.asa.org.uk/Adjudications/sh...d=all&from_index=by_sector&sector_id=2> (accessed 11 March 2002).

Alvesson, Mats (1994) 'Talking in organizations: managing identity and impressions in an advertising agency', *Organization Studies*, **15** (4): 535–63.

Amos, Amanda (1992) *Style and Image: Tobacco and Alcohol Images*, London: Health Education Authority.

Appadurai, Arjun (1986) 'Introduction: commodities and the politics of value', in Arjun Appadurai (ed.) *The Social Life of Things: Commodities in Cultural Perspective*, Cambridge: Cambridge University Press.

Arlen, Michael J. (1980) *Thirty Seconds*, New York: Farrar, Straus and Giroux.

Asendorf, Christoph (1993) *Batteries of Life: On the History of Things and their Perception in Modernity*, trans. Don Reneau, Berkeley: University of California Press.

Barthes, Roland (1974) *Mythologies*, trans. Annette Lavers, London: Jonathan Cape.

Baudelaire, Charles (1961) *Oeuvres Complètes*, ed. Claude Pichois, Paris: Éditions Gallimard.

Baudrillard, Jean (1988) *Selected Writings*, ed. Mark Poster, Oxford: Polity Press.

Beattie, Alan (1991) 'Knowledge and control in health promotion: a test case for social policy and social theory', in Jonathan Gabe, Michael Calnan and Michael Bury (eds) *The Sociology of the Health Service*, London: Routledge.

Beck, Ulrich (1992) *Risk Society: Towards a New Modernity*, trans. Mark Ritter, London: Sage.

Benjamin, Walter (1973) *Charles Baudelaire: A Lyric Poet in the Era of High Capitalism*, trans. Harry Zohn, London: NLB.

Berlant, Lauren (2002) Comments at 'The archive and the object' workshop, 19 June, Lancaster University, UK.

Berridge, Virginia and Edwards, Griffith (1987) *Opium and the People: Opiate Use in Nineteenth Century England*, New Haven and London: Yale University Press.

Boddewyn, Jean J. (1992) *Global Perspectives on Advertising Self-Regulation: Principles and Practices in 38 Countries*, Westport, CT: Quorum Books.

Bourdieu, Pierre (2000 [1984]) *Distinction: A Social Critique of the Judgement of Taste*, trans. Richard Nice, London: Routledge.

Bowlby, Rachel (1985) *Just Looking: Consumer Culture in Dreiser, Gissing and Zola*, London: Routledge.

—— (1993) *Shopping With Freud*, London: Routledge.

—— (2000) *Carried Away: The Invention of Modern Shopping*, London: Faber and Faber.

Brierley, Sean (1995) *The Advertising Handbook*, London: Routledge.

Briggs, Asa (1988) *Victorian Things*, London: B.T. Batsford Ltd.

Broadcast Advertising Clearance Centre (1999) *Pre-Transmission Clearance for Television Advertising*. Online. Available HTTP: <http://www.bacc.org.uk/li...0419875FA8025 6A6500541D2A?OpenDocument> (accessed 25 August 2001).

Bullmore, Jeremy (1991) *Behind the Scenes in Advertising*, Henley-on-Thames: NTC Publications Ltd.

Burnett, John (1999) *Liquid Pleasures: A Social History of Drinks in Modern Britain*, London: Routledge.

Butler, Judith (1993) *Bodies That Matter: On the Discursive Limits of 'Sex'*, London: Routledge.

Calfee, John E. (1997) *Fear of Persuasion: A New Perspective on Advertising and Regulation*, Monnaz: Agora.

Camhi, Leslie (1993) 'Stealing femininity: department store kleptomania as sexual disorder', *Differences*, 5 (1): 26–50.

Campbell, Colin (1987) *The Romantic Ethic and the Spirit of Modern Consumerism*, Oxford and New York: Blackwell.

Campbell, Nancy D. (2000) *Using Women: Gender, Drug Policy, and Social Justice*, London: Routledge.

Clark, Eric (1990) *The Want Makers: Inside the World of Advertising*, London: Penguin.

Clarke, Alison (2000) '"Mother swapping": the trafficking of nearly new children's wear', in Peter Jackson, Daniel Miller and Frank Mort (eds) *Commercial Cultures: Economies, Practices, Spaces*, Oxford: Berg.

Cohn, Tom (1998) *Ideology and Inscription: 'Cultural Studies' After Benjamin, de Man, and Bakhtin*, Cambridge: Cambridge University Press.

Coombe, Rosemary J. (1998) *The Cultural Life of Intellectual Properties: Authorship, Appropriation, and the Law*, Durham, NC and London: Duke University Press.

Craig, Steve and Moellinger, Terry (2001) '"So rich, mild, and fresh": a critical look at TV cigarette commercials, 1948–1971', *Journal of Communication Inquiry*, **25** (Jan.): 55–71.

Cronin, Anne M. (2000a) *Advertising and Consumer Citizenship: Gender, Images and Rights*, London: Routledge.

—— (2000b) 'Consumerism and "compulsory individuality": women, will and potential', in Sara Ahmed, Jane Kilby, Celia Lury, Maureen McNeil and Beverley Skeggs (eds) *Transformations: Thinking Through Feminism*, London: Routledge.

—— (2002a) 'The substance of consumption: alchemy, addiction and the commodity', *International Journal of Cultural Studies*, **5** (3): 316–35.

—— (2002b) 'Consumer rights/cultural rights: a new politics of European belonging', *European Journal of Cultural Studies*, **5** (3): 307–23.

Cross, Gary (2001) 'Corralling consumer culture: shifting rationales for American state intervention in free markets', in Martin Daunton and Matthew Hilton (eds) *The Politics of Consumption: Material Culture and Citizenship in Europe and America*, Oxford: Berg.

Crossick, Geoffrey and Jaumain, Serge (1999) 'The world of the department store: distribution, culture and social change', in Geoffrey Crossick and Serge Jaumain (eds) *Cathedrals of Consumption: The European Department Store, 1850–1939*, Aldershot: Ashgate.

Dally, Ann (1995) 'Anomalies and mysteries in the 'War on Drugs', in Roy Porter and Mikuláš Teich (eds) *Drugs and Narcotics in History*, Cambridge: Cambridge University Press.

Davidson, Martin (1992) *The Consumerist Manifesto: Advertising in Postmodern Times*, London: Routledge.

Debord, Guy (1994 [1967]) *The Society of the Spectacle*, trans. Donald Nicholson-Smith, New York: Zone Books.

Deleuze, Gilles (1995) *Negotiations, 1972–1990*, trans. Martin Joughin, New York: Columbia University Press.

Department of Health (2002) *Tobacco Advertising and Promotion Bill Consultation Document*. Online. Available HTTP: <http://www.doh.gov.uk/tobaccoregsconsult/index.htm> (accessed 16 September 2002).

Derrida, Jacques (1981) *Dissemination*, trans. Barbara Johnson, London: Athlone Press.

—— (1993) 'The rhetoric of drugs: an interview', *Differences*, **5** (1): 1–25.

Diprose, Rosalyn (1994) *The Bodies of Women: Ethics, Embodiment and Sexual Difference*, London: Routledge

Douglas, Mary (1992) *Risk and Blame: Essays in Cultural Theory*, London: Routledge.

Douglas, Mary and Isherwood, Baron (1979) *The World of Goods: Towards an Anthropology of Consumption*, London: Allen Lane.

Elliott, Blanche B. (1962) *A History of English Advertising*, London: Business Publications Ltd. In association with B.T. Batsford.

Elster, John and Skog, Ole-Jørgen (eds) (1999) *Getting Hooked: Rationality and Addiction*, Cambridge: Cambridge University Press.

European Commission (2001) *Directive on the Advertising of Tobacco Products and Related Sponsorship*. Online. Available HTTP: <http://www.doh.gov.uk/adtobacco.htm> (accessed 10 August 2001).

Ewen, Stuart (1988) *All Consuming Images: The Politics of Style in Contemporary Culture*, New York: Basic Books.

Ewick, Patricia (1993) 'Corporate cures: the commodification of social control', *Studies in Law, Politics and Society*, **13**: 137–57.

Falk, Pasi (1997) 'The genealogy of advertising', in Pekka Sulkunen, John Holmwood, Hilary Radner and Gerhard Schulze (eds) *Constructing the New Consumer Society*, Basingstoke: Macmillan.

Falk, Pasi and Campbell, Colin (eds) (1997) *The Shopping Experience*, London: Sage.

Featherstone, Mike (1991) *Consumer Culture and Postmodernism*, London: Sage.

Felski, Rita (1995) *The Gender of Modernity*, Cambridge, MA and London: Harvard University Press.

Finnegan, Margaret (1999) *Selling Suffrage: Consumer Culture and Votes for Women*, New York: Columbia University Press.

Fletcher, Winston (1999) *Advertising Advertising*, London: Profile Books.

Foucault, Michel (1980) 'Truth and power', in Colin Gordon (ed.) *Power/Knowledge. Selected Interviews and Other Writings 1972–1977*, trans. Colin Gordon, Leo Marshall, John Mepham, Kate Soper, London: Harvester Press.

—— (1990a) *The History of Sexuality: Vol. 1, An Introduction*, trans. Robert Hurley, London: Penguin.

—— (1990b) *The History of Sexuality: Vol. 3, The Care of the Self*, trans. Robert Hurley, London: Penguin.

—— (1990c) 'The dangerous individual', in Lawrence Kritzman (ed.) (1990) *Michel Foucault: Politics, Philosophy, Culture. Interviews and Other Writings 1977–1984*, trans. Alan Sheridan, London: Routledge.

—— (1990d) 'Practising criticism', in Lawrence Kritzman (ed.) *Michel Foucault: Politics, Philosophy, Culture. Interviews and Other Writings 1977–1984*, trans. Alan Sheridan, London: Routledge.

—— (1991) *Discipline and Punish: The Birth of the Prison*, trans. Alan Sheridan, London: Penguin.

—— (2000a) *The Birth of the Clinic: An Archaeology of Medical Perception*, trans. Alan Sheridan, London: Routledge.

—— (2000b) *The Order of Things: An Archaeology of the Human Sciences*, London: Routledge.

—— (2001) *The Archaeology of Knowledge*, trans. Alan Sheridan Smith, London: Routledge.

Fowles, Jib (1996) *Advertising and Popular Culture*, London: Sage.

Franklin, Sarah, Lury, Celia and Stacey, Jackie (2000) *Global Nature, Global Culture*, London: Sage.

Fraser, Nancy and Gordon, Linda (1997) 'A genealogy of "dependency": tracing a keyword of the U.S. Welfare State', in Nancy Fraser *Justice Interruptus: Critical Reflections on the 'Postsocialist' Condition*, London and New York: Routledge.

Fraser, W. Hamish (1981) *The Coming of the Mass Market, 1850–1914*, London and Basingstoke: Macmillan Press.

Friedberg, Anne (1993) *Window Shopping: Cinema and the Postmodern*, Berkeley: University of California Press.

Gabriel, Yiannis and Lang, Tim (1995) *The Unmanageable Consumer: Contemporary Consumption and its Fragmentations*, London: Sage.

Galbraith, J. K. (1958) *The Affluent Society*, Boston: Houghton Mifflin.

Garvey, Ellen Gruber (1996) *The Adman in the Parlor: Magazines and the Gendering of Consumer Culture, 1880s to 1910s*, Oxford: Oxford University Press.

Goldman, Robert (1992) *Reading Ads Socially*, London: Routledge.

Goodwin, Christopher (2002) 'Millions died because of me', Online. Available HTTP: <http://www.timesonline.co.uk/article/0,,7-325745,00.html> (accessed 24 June 2002).

Gosden, Chris and Knowles, Chantal (2001) *Collecting Colonialism: Material Culture and Colonial Change*, Oxford: Berg.

Hacking, Ian (1990) *The Taming of Chance*, Cambridge: Cambridge University Press.

Hallam, Elizabeth and Hockey, Jenny (2001) *Death, Memory and Material Culture*, Oxford: Berg.

Hallam, Elizabeth, Hockey, Jenny, Howarth, Glennys (1999) *Beyond the Body: Death and Social Identity*, London: Routledge.

Haraway, Donna J. (1991) *Simians, Cyborgs and Women: The Reinvention of Nature*, London: Free Association Books.

—— (1997) *Modest_Witness@Second_Millennium.FemaleMan©_Meets_OncoMouse™*, London and New York: Routledge.

Hastings, Gerard and MacFadyen, Lynn (2000a) 'A day in the life of an advertising man: review of internal documents from the UK tobacco industry's principal advertising agencies', *British Medical Journal*, **321**: 366–71.

—— (2000b) *Keep Smiling. No One's Going to Die: An Analysis of Internal Documents From the Tobacco Industry's Main UK Advertising Agencies*, London: British Medical Association.

Haug, Wolfgang Fritz (1986) *Critique of Commodity Aesthetics: Appearance, Sexuality and Advertising in Capitalist Society*, trans. Robert Bock, Minneapolis: University of Minnesota Press.

Health Select Committee (2000) *Second Report on the Tobacco Industry and the Health Risks of Smoking*, October, command paper, Cm 4905.

High, Hugh (1999) *Does Advertising Increase Smoking? Economics, Free Speech and Advertising Bans*, London: The Institute for Economic Affairs.

Hirota, Janice M. (1995) 'Making products heroes: work in advertising agencies', in Robert Jackall (ed.) *Propaganda*, Basingstoke: Macmillan.

Hower, Ralph M. (1949) *The History of an Advertising Agency: N.W. Ayer and Son at Work 1869–1949*, Cambridge, MA: Harvard University Press.

Incorporated Society of British Advertisers (2001) *About Us*. Online. Available HTTP: <http://www.isba.org.uk/about_us/index.html> (accessed 25 August 2001).

Independent Television Commission (1998) *ITC Code of Advertising Standards and Practice*. Online. Available HTTP: <http://www.itc.org.uk/regulating/ad_spons/index.asp> (accessed 20 August 2001).

—— (2001) *ITC Complaints Reports, January 2001*. Online. Available HTTP: <http://www.itc.org.uk/divisions/ad_spons...ws&date=January+2001&ad_complaint_id =482> (accessed 20 August 2001).

Institute of Alcohol Studies (2001) *Marketing Alcohol to Young People – An Industry Out of Control*. Online. Available HTTP: <http://www.ias.org.uk/pressreleases.htm> (accessed 10 August 2001).

Jackall, Robert and Hirota, Janice (2000) *Image Makers: Advertising, Public Relations and the Ethos of Advocacy*, Chicago: University of Chicago Press.

Jenkins, Philip (1999) *Synthetic Panics: The Symbolic Politics of Designer Drugs*, New York and London: New York University Press.

Jhally, Sut (1987) *The Codes of Advertising: Fetishism and the Political Economy of Meaning in Consumer Society*, London: Frances Pinter.

Keane, Helen (2002) *What's Wrong With Addiction?* New York: New York University Press.

Kenny, Ursula (2001) 'Hooked on addiction', *Observer* (18 February). Online. Available HTTP: <hhttp://www.observer.co.uk/life/story/0,6903,439431,00.html> (accessed 16 May 2001).

Kluger, Richard (1996) *Ashes to Ashes: America's Hundred-Year Cigarette War, the Public Health, and the Unabashed Triumph of Philip Morris*, New York: Alfred A. Knopf.

Kohn, Marek (1992) *Dope Girls: The Birth of the British Drug Underground*, London: Lawrence and Wishart.

Kopytoff, Igor (1986) 'The cultural biography of things: commoditization as process', in Arjun Appadurai (ed.) *The Social Life of Things: Commodities in Cultural Perspective*, Cambridge: Cambridge University Press.

Kover, Arthur J. and Goldberg, Stephen M. (1995) 'The games copywriters play: conflict, quasi-control, a new proposal', *Journal of Advertising Research*, **35** (4): 52–62.

Kritzman, Lawrence (ed.) (1990) *Michel Foucault: Politics, Philosophy, Culture. Interviews and Other Writings 1977–1984*, London: Routledge.

Laird, Pamela Walker (1998) *Advertising Progress: American Business and the Rise of Consumer Marketing*, Baltimore and London: Johns Hopkins University Press.

Lash, Scott and Urry, John (1994) *Economies of Signs and Space*, London: Sage.

Latour, Bruno (1993) *We Have Never Been Modern*, trans. Catherine Porter, Hemel Hempstead: Prentice Hall/Harvester Wheatsheaf.

Law, John and Benschop, Ruth (1997) 'Resisting pictures: representation, distribution and ontological politics', in Kevin Hetherington and Rolland Munro (eds) *Ideas of Difference: Social Spaces and the Labour of Division*, Oxford: Blackwell/The Sociological Review.

Leach, William (1989) 'Strategists of display and the production of desire', in Simon J. Bronner (ed.) *Consuming Visions: Accumulation and Display of Goods in America, 1880–1920*, London and New York: W.W. Norton and Company.

Lears, Jackson (1983) 'From salvation to self-realization: advertising and the therapeutic roots of consumer culture, 1880–1930', in Richard Wightman Fox and T.J. Jackson Lears (eds) *The Culture of Consumption: Critical Essays in American History, 1880–1980*, New York: Pantheon Books.

—— (1994) *Fables of Abundance: A Cultural History of Advertising in America*, New York: Basic Books.

Lee, Martyn J. (1993) *Consumer Culture Reborn: The Cultural Politics of Consumption*, London: Routledge.

Leiss, William (1978) *The Limits to Satisfaction: On Needs and Commodities*, London: Marion Boyars.

Leiss, William, Kline, Stephen, Jhally, Sut (1990) *Social Communication in Advertising: Persons, Products and Images of Well-Being*, 2nd edn, London: Routledge.

Lenson, David (1995) *On Drugs*, Minneapolis and London: University of Minnesota Press.

Lievrouw, L.A. (1994) 'Health communication research reconsidered: reading the signs', *Journal of Communication*, **44** (1): 90–9.

Loeb, Lori Anne (1994) *Consuming Angels: Advertising and Victorian Women*, Oxford: Oxford University Press.

Lupton, Deborah (1995) *The Imperative of Health: Public Health and the Regulated Body*, London: Sage.

Lury, Celia (1993) *Cultural Rights: Technology, Legality and Personality*, London: Routledge.

Lury, Celia and Warde, Alan (1997) 'Investments in the imaginary consumer: conjectures regarding power, knowledge and advertising', in Mica Nava, Andrew Blake, Iain MacRury and Barry Richards (eds) *Buy This Book: Studies in Advertising and Consumption*, London: Routledge.

McClintock, Anne (1995) *Imperial Leather: Race, Gender and Sexuality in the Colonial Contest*, London: Routledge.

McDonald, Maryon (1994) 'Introduction: a social-anthropological view of gender, drink and drugs', in Maryon McDonald (ed.) *Gender, Drink and Drugs*, Oxford: Berg.

McFall, Liz (2000) 'A mediating institution?: Using an historical study of advertising practice to rethink culture and economy', *Cultural Values*, **4** (3): 314–38.

McVeigh, Tracey (2000) 'One woman in five is a shopaholic', the *Observer*. Online. Available HTTP: <http://www.observer.co.uk/uk_news/story/0,6903,403121,00.html> (accessed 16 May 2001).

Maibach, Edward and Parrott, Roxanne Louiselle (eds) (1995) *Designing Health Messages: Approaches from Communicaion Theory and Public Health Practice*, London: Sage.

Marchand, Roland (1985) *Advertising the American Dream: Making Way for Modernity, 1920–1940*, Berkeley and London: University of California Press.

Marx, Karl (1970) *Economic and Philosophic Manuscripts of 1844*, trans. Martin Milligan, London: Lawrence and Wishart.

—— (1978) *Grundrisse: Foundations of the Critique of Political Economy*, trans. Martin Nicolaus, London: Allen Lane in association with New Left Review.

—— (1990) *Capital, Vol. 1*, intro. Ernest Mandel, trans. Ben Fowkes, Harmondsworth: Penguin Classics.

—— (1992) *Early Writings*, intro. Lucio Colletti, trans. Rodney Livingstone and Gregor Benton, London: Penguin Classics.

Mattelart, Armand (1991) *Advertising International: The Privatisation of Public Space*; trans. Michael Channan, London: Routledge.

Miller, Daniel (1987) *Material Culture and Mass Consumption*, Oxford: Blackwell.

—— (1997) *Capitalism: An Ethnographic Approach*, Oxford: Berg.

—— (1998) *A Theory of Shopping*, Cambridge: Polity Press.

—— (2001) *The Dialectics of Shopping*, Chicago and London: University of Chicago Press.

—— (2002) 'The unintended political economy', in Du Gay, Paul and Pryke, Michael (eds) *Cultural Economy: Cultural Analysis and Commercial Life*, London: Sage.

Miller, Michael B. (1981) *The Bon Marché: Bourgeois Culture and the Department Store, 1869–1920*, Princeton, NJ: Princeton University Press.

Mintz, Sidney W. (1993) 'The changing role of food in the study of consumption', in John Brewer and Roy Porter (eds) *Consumption and the World of Goods*, London: Routledge.

Moeran, Brian (1996) *A Japanese Advertising Agency: An Anthropology of Media and Markets*, Richmond: Curzon.

Mort, Frank (1996) *Cultures of Consumption: Masculinities and Social Space in Late Twentieth-Century Britain*, London: Routledge.

Nava, Mica (1997) 'Framing advertising', in Mica Nava, Andrew Blake, Iain MacRury and Barry Richards (eds) *Buy This Book: Studies in Advertising and Consumption*, London: Routledge.

Nevett, T.R. (1982) *Advertising in Britain: A History*, London: Heinemann.

Nixon, Sean (1996) *Hard Looks: Masculinities, Spectatorship and Contemporary Consumption*, London: UCL Press.

—— (2000) 'In pursuit of the professional ideal: advertising and the construction of commercial expertise in Britain 1953–64', in Peter Jackson, Daniel Miller and Frank Mort (eds) *Commercial Cultures: Economies, Practices, Spaces*, Oxford: Berg.

—— (2002) 'Re-imagining the ad agency: the cultural connotations of economic forms', in Paul du Gay and Michael Pryke (eds) *Cultural Economy: Cultural Analysis and Commercial Life*, London: Sage.

O'Brien, Patricia (1983) 'The kleptomania diagnosis: bourgeois women and theft in late nineteenth century France', *Journal of Social History*, **17**: 65–77.

O'Connor, Erin (2000) *Raw Material: Producing Pathology in Victorian Culture*, Durham, NC and London: Duke University Press.

Ogilvy, David (1964) *Confessions of an Advertising Man*, London: Longmans, Green and Co.

—— (1983) *Ogilvy on Advertising*, London: Pan Books.

Ohmann, Richard (1996) *Selling Culture: Magazines, Markets, and Class at the Turn of the Century*, London and New York: Verso.

Olalquiaga, Celeste (1999) *The Artificial Kingdom: A Treasury of Kitsch Experience*, London: Bloomsbury.

Otis, Laura (1994) *Organic Memory: History and the Body in Late Nineteenth and Early Twentieth Centuries*, Lincoln, NE and London: University of Nebraska Press.

Packard, Vance (1957) *The Hidden Persuaders*, London: David MacKay.

Palmer, Camilla (2001) 'Does advertising have a conscience?', *Campaign*, 21 September: 22–3.

Pateman, Carole (1988) *The Sexual Contract*, Oxford: Blackwell.

Pattison, Stephen and Player, David (1990) 'Health education: the political tensions', in Spyros Doxiadis (ed.) *Ethics in Health Education*, Chichester: John Wiley and Sons.

Pearce, Susan, M. (1992) *Museums, Objects and Collections*, Washington, DC: Smithsonian Instition Press.

—— (1994) *Museums and the Appropriation of Culture*, London: Athlone Press.

—— (1995) *On Collecting: An Investigation into Collecting in the European Tradition*, London: Routledge.

Pease, Otis (1958) *The Responsibilities of American Advertising: Private Control and Public Influence, 1920–1940*, New Haven: Yale University Press.

Pels, Peter (1998) 'The spirit of the matter: on fetish, rarity, fact and fancy', in Patricia Spyer (ed.) *Border Fetishisms: Material Objects in Unstable Spaces*, London: Routledge.

Pinch, Adela (1998) 'Stealing happiness: shoplifting in early nineteenth-century England', in Patricia Spyer (ed.) *Border Fetishisms: Material Objects in Unstable Spaces*, London: Routledge.

Pope, Daniel (1983) *The Making of Modern Advertising*, New York: Basic Books.

Porter, Roy (1989) *Health For Sale: Quackery in England 1660–1850*, Manchester: Manchester University Press.

—— (1993) 'Consumption: disease of the consumer society?', in John Brewer and Roy Porter (eds) *Consumption and the World of Goods*, London and New York: Routledge.

Presbrey, Frank (1929) *The History and Development of Advertising*, New York: Doubleday, Doran and Company.

Rabinbach, Anson (1992) *The Human Motor: Energy, Fatigue, and the Origins of Modernity*, Berkeley: University of California Press.

abiner, Karen (1993) *Inventing Desire: Inside Chiat/Day, the Hottest Shop, the Coolest Players, the Big Business of Advertising*, New York: Simon and Schuster.

allybrass, Peter (1998) 'Marx's coat', in Patricia Spyer (ed.) *Border Fetishisms: Material Objects in Unstable Spaces*, London: Routledge.

ewart, Susan (1993) *On Longing: Narratives of the Miniature, the Gigantic, the Souvenir, the Collection*, Durham, NC and London: Duke University Press.

athern, Marilyn (1999) *Property, Substance and Effect: Anthropological Essays on Persons and Things*, London and New Brunswick, NJ: Athlone.

ussig, Michael (1992) *The Nervous System*, London: Routledge.

om, Betsy (1994) 'Women and alcohol: the emergence of a risk group', in Maryon McDonald (ed.) *Gender, Drink and Drugs*, Oxford: Berg.

rsten, Lisa (1999) 'Marianne in the department store: gender and the politics of consumption in turn-of-the-century Paris', in Geoffrey Crossick and Serge Jaumain (eds) *Cathedrals of Consumption: The European Department Store, 1850–1939*, Aldershot: Ashgate.

— (2001) *Marianne in The Market: Envisioning Consumer Society in Fin-de-Siècle France*, Berkeley and London: University of California Press.

acco Manufacturers Association (2001) *The TMA: Introduction*. Online. Available TTP: <http://www.thetma.org.uk/miscellaneous/introduction.htm> (accessed 31 ugust 2001).

ch, John and Lupton, Deborah (1997) *Television, AIDS and Risk: A Cultural Studies pproach to Health Communication*, St Leonards: Allen and Unwin.

all, Jeremy (1964) *The Advertising Man in London Advertising Agencies*, London: apman and Hall Ltd.

r, E.S. (1965) *The Shocking History of Advertising*, Harmondsworth: Penguin in sociation with Michael Joseph.

overnment (1998) *Smoking Kills*. Online. Available HTTP: <http://www.official-uments.co.uk/cgi...RDS=advertis+tobacco&COLOUR=Red&STYLE=s> (accessed August 2001).

(2001) *Tobacco Advertising and Promotion Bill*. Online. Available HTTP: p://www.parliament.the-stationery-off...o.uk/pa/ld200102/ldbills/007/2002007.htm> essed 10 August 2001).

de, Mariana (1997) '"Slavery from within": the invention of alcoholism and the tion of free will', *Social History*, **22** (3): 251–68.

998) *Diseases of the Will: Alcohol and the Dilemmas of Freedom*, Cambridge: bridge University Press.

, Andrew (1991) *Promotional Culture: Advertising, Ideology and Symbolic ession*, London: Sage.

Carolyn (1990) *Women Who Shop Too Much: Overcoming the Urge to Splurge*, York: St Martin's Press.

, Raymond (1980) *Problems in Materialism and Culture*, London: NLB.

, Rosalind (1982) *Dream Worlds: Mass Consumption in Late Nineteenth-Century e*, Berkeley and London: University of California Press.

on, Judith (2000) *Decoding Advertisements: Ideology and Meaning in Advertising*, n: Marion Boyars.

net (1995) *Resident Alien: Feminist Cultural Criticism*, Cambridge: Polity

nk (1999) *Curbing the Epidemic: Governments and the Economics of Tobacco l*, Washington, DC: The World Bank in association with WHO.

Rappaport, Erika D. (2000) *Shopping For Pleasure: Women in the M*
West End, Princeton, NJ and Chichester: Princeton University Pr(

Reekie, Gail (1993) *Temptations: Sex, Selling and the Departmer*
Australia: Allen and Unwin.

Richards, Thomas (1990) *The Commodity Culture of Victorian Eng*
Spectacle 1851–1914, London: Verso.

Ronell, Avital (1992) *Crack Wars: Literature, Addiction, Mania*, Li
University of Nebraska Press.

—— (1993) 'Our narcotic modernity', in Verena Andermatt (
Technologies, Minneapolis and London: University of Minnes(

Rose, Nikolas (1996) *Inventing Our Selves: Psychology, P(*
Cambridge: Cambridge University Press.

Sahlins, Marshall (1976) *Culture and Practical Reason*, Chicag(
of Chicago Press.

Saisselin, Rémy G. (1985) *Bricabracomania: The Bourgeois*
Thames and Hudson.

Schudson, Michael (1993) *Advertising, the Uneasy Persuasi(*
American Society, London: Routledge.

Schwartz, Hillel (1986) *Never Satisfied: A Cultural History o*
New York: The Free Press.

—— (1989) 'The three-body problem and the end of the w(
Fragments for a History of the Human Body: Part Two, N(

Sedgwick, Eve K. (1994) *Tendencies*, London: Routledge.

Select Committee on Health (2000) *The Tobacco Industry an(*
(TB 28). Online. Available HTTP: <http://www.parliamen
cmselect/cmhealth/27/0011313.html> (accessed 10 Augu

Seltzer, Mark (1992) *Bodies and Machines*, London: Routle(

—— (1993) 'Serial killers (1)', *Differences*, **5** (1): 92–128.

—— (1998) *Serial Killers: Death and Life in America's Wou(*

Sheller, Mimi (2000) *Democracy After Slavery: Black Pub*
Haiti and Jamaica, London: Macmillan.

—— (2003) *Consuming the Caribbean: From Arawaks to*

Sivulka, Juliann (1998) *Soap, Sex, and Cigarettes: A*
Advertising, Belmont, CA: Wadsworth.

Skeggs, Beverley (1997) *Formations of Class and Gender:*
Sage.

Slater, Don (1989) 'Corridors of power' in Jaber F. Gub
The Politics of Field Research: Sociology Beyond En

—— (2003) 'Markets, materiality and the "new econc
Warde (eds) *Market Relations and the Competitive*
University Press.

Soar, Matthew (2000) 'Encoding advertisements: ide
production', *Mass Communication and Society*, **3** (*

Spiekermann, Uwe (1999) 'Theft and thieves in Germ
discourse on morality, crime and gender', in Geoffr
Cathedrals of Consumption: The European Depar
Ashgate.

Spivak, Gayatri Chakravorty (1987) *In Other Worlds:*
and London: Methuen.

World Health Organization (2000) *Framework Convention on Tobacco Control.* Online. Available HTTP: <http://tobacco.who.int/en/fctc/index.html> (accessed 10 August 2001).
—— (2001) *Member States Need to Take Action Against Tobacco Advertising.* Online. Available HTTP: <http://www.who.int/inf-pr-2001/en/pr2001-47.html> (accessed 18 January 2002).

Index